895

EDEN

D0290889

EDEN

Poems by
Dennis Schmitz

UNIVERSITY
OF ILLINOIS PRESS
URBANA AND
CHICAGO

Publication of this work was supported in part by grants from the National Endowment for the Arts and the Illinois Arts Council, a state agency.

©1989 by Dennis Schmitz
Manufactured in the United States of America
P   5   4   3   2   1

This book is printed on acid-free paper.

Library of Congress Cataloging-in-Publication Data

Schmitz, Dennis, 1937–
    Eden : poems / by Dennis Schmitz.
      p. cm.
    ISBN 0-252-06050-4 (alk. paper)
    I. Title.
PS3569.C517E34 1989
811'.54—dc 19   88-23526
                       CIP

These poems have appeared in the following magazines, to whose editors grateful acknowledgment is made:

American Poetry Review
"U.S. Considers War with Libya" (17, no. 6 [1988])
"Good Friday" (17, no. 6 [1988])
"Halloween" (17, no. 6 [1988])
"Sterno" (17, no. 6 [1988])
"Zoo" (17, no. 6 [1988])

Antaeus
"Instructions for Fishing the Eel" (Autumn, 1985; rpt., *The Antaeus Anthology,* ed. Daniel Halpern)

California Quarterly
"Blue" (Winter, 1987)
"The Spider" (Winter, 1987)

Field
"Hunting" (no. 31)
"Bird-Watching" (Spring, 1987; rpt., *The Longman Anthology of Contemporary American Poetry,* 2d ed., and *Pushcart Prize XIII*)
"Harness" (Spring, 1988)
"Driving with One Light" (Fall, 1985)
"Halloween Creature" (Spring, 1987)
"The Grand Egress" (Spring, 1988)
"Ladder" (Spring, 1984)
"So High" (Fall, 1984)
"Eden" (Fall, 1984)

Five Finger Review
"Matthew's Lesson" (no. 3)

Hayden's Ferry Review
"Catfishing" (Spring, 1989)

Mt. Aukum Review
"The Pour" (nos. 2-3)

Pacific Review
    "Climbing Sears Tower"

Poetry Now
    "Instructions for Rowing"

Tendril
    "La Traviata" (nos. 14–15)

Tri-Quarterly
    "Chicago: State & Van Buren" (Spring/Summer, 1984;
    appeared originally as "State & Van Buren")
    "The Apparatus"

I wish to thank the National Endowment for the Arts for a grant
supporting the writing of this book, California State University
(Sacramento) University Research Committee and the Univer-
sity Office of Research and Sponsored Projects for grants, and
the Poetry Society of America for the annual di Castagnola Award
given the book manuscript.

for Nick & Josephine D'Agostino,
second parents

Contents

PART I

Hunting

Hunting the October river ochre
& so low the currents fuse
in popple & berry canes,

Dad, I & a nervy retriever
do a cautious hunt-dance,
stepping ataxic, thigh-high steps
where the mud clots

to form birds.
We are following the dog,
progressively losing ourselves
to leaf & the random

weed patterns pheasants use —
a camouflage so complete
we are the only things that aren't

part of its parts.
The sun should show us
where we are in the overwhelming

fecundity of the visible,
but the dog decides
how we stoop, hug past stickers

& not look. Maybe we don't even think
"birds" until my father
says *shoot*
against the sky where the bird is all

outline & hands me the gun.
When I won't, he shoots late—
the second bird whirrs
into a shot-pattern so palpable my eyes prickle

& tear. My father swipes at the dog,
pulls away wing pieces,
punches the dog's head, but it won't let go

the ratty feathers looped in spittle.
I'm eleven; later I understand
the dead clamped in a bloody aurora,

a dog's mouth,
that sometimes is sweet—
it'll nip the grass to clean its taste

& vow never to defect
to appetite,
though it licks your arm

&, asking caresses, leaves a streak
of blood.

Instructions for Fishing the Eel

for Ray Carver

December pools, latent, crosshatched
    in low wind
& the rest of the stream all exegesis.
Steelhead will nose
the water-seams around rocks
    where you can drop

yarn-flies or a roe-dip compound
    that bleeds red taste
around your hook,
    the fog head-high & bleeding too

out of nearby firs
hooked down by the same ice
    you sometimes pull through your reel
in stiff, small O's that mean
    you've lost all weight

at the line's end: your connection,
    your tie to the it-world.
Your second lesson: when a fish
twists, leaps through

to our world to throw hook
    or die, contention stops—
where the line enters water
    is equipoise,
centering: fish & human at last
    in balance & glorying,

if either can, in the other.
& last lesson: the steelhead's context
        is ocean; the hardest
lesson is to let go

what one can't be, first immersing
        the releasing hand,
dirtied by bait
but dry enough paradoxically to slime
        off in rainbows
the fish's protective coat: the hand's

reward is to feel
the no-shape of water, feel human warmth
drain away in the wetting.

Bird-Watching

Across the channel, Mare Island welders cut
bulkheads & winch up
riveted slabs of the WW II

mine-tender. I can see
the torches flash against visualized rust;
I can see so far
back that the war cruelties are camouflaged

as feats of scruple.
The binoculars sweat rings around my eyes,
& when my arms tire, it's the sky that comes down

fuzzy through the Zeiss
26 × 10 lens into debris—the shoe, paper news
& condoms, the "beauty

from brevity derived" I can't catalog.
I'm on the flyway for marbled
godwits, scooters & loons,
but taxidermy might have devised what I think

is only a dead heron peppered with grit,
marshgrass poking
out the bird's buggy eyeholes.
I want to get down,
include myself in the focus: the war,

all epithets, between memory & present things
memory can't yet reach.
Though the marsh is a constant

madras-bleed between old soda bottles
that slash grids in the earthbound
walker's boots & the heuristic dieback

of the grass, I'm on one knee
to this Bird-in-the-volleys-of-lesser-birds,
praising glut but lifting
binoculars once more to distance myself

from it. Idolatry begins in one's fear
of being the only thing, saying, for example,
to detritus, *let it linger, let even just the feathers*

of it stay—that is why I pick
up my glasses with the little men still in them.
They are so intent on forgetting;

they are so self-contained & innocent,
lit both by the binoculars' small
circles of sky & by the torches the men stroke
against the steel that arches over them.

U.S. Considers War with Libya

The rowboat sets out
over pollen-clogged twilight
so clogged that
water is a linguistic distinction,

a subconscious that wants to push
up through the message—
that's why my oars catch,

that's why I can go forward
over suicide-by-drowning.
I've helped myself by saying
I'm rowing the seven missionaries
cannibals pursue through
the algebra problem: how many trips

& myself safe with them on the nether side?
By now I'm at least the Keats
of the paramecium & pond toad,
swallowing yellow but scaring off the circling

scissortails who feed mouths wide
by opening my own mouth to song which fits
approximately their state.
I puzzle out what I mean by "shore"

as the cannibals would puzzle while they eat
the missionary I couldn't save—
"shore" is his fear that they savor,

acid yet so sweet.
In the Chinese lament, there's a soldier pissing
in the river as Li Po's poems sink,
but the soldier's so far upriver that relief from war,

not the taint, is the poem's concern.
For example: no matter how often the president looks
into the mirror & sees Khadafy,

he isn't Li Po drowning
as he tries to embrace his own reflection.
I feather the oars
but clumsily; I want so to let myself drift.

Harness

26 years married luckily
each to the other's eros, you & I,
but our friends who married

only for context
or for patience with a sexual prey
find desire an irresolute

prayer that weeps for itself.
Not a Lamia, not small Keats's lack
by which she was made hungry for men—

even a woman who loved women,
the '20s painter Romaine Brooks,
drew humans in disciplinary blacks
evolving out of animals

in the lower parts of their clothes.
Each seems open to the trespass—
they're like the thieves in Dante's hell

who forever change
from humans to beasts to humans they've affixed
themselves to because they have

no sense of self.
Does one give up to fury for love
equal to it & go lost

into somewhere black
as the IRT station, led by the other's surrender
like the woman we once saw guiding
her blind husband by clinging to a harness

of canvas she probably made,
in tandem going down the subway stairs,
steering him around dogshit trampled

into incipience,
the loose floor tiles,
the dangers she must become impetuous for—
just barely before the uptown train rockets

to them, the wife slaps
down his endangered arm.

Good Friday

First the procession representing
what could destroy us,
then the flagellants raising welts on one another
in praise of it—
then, *hosanna,* the warty New Mexico gourds,

the strings of chilis.
My Volvo is out with the other Volvos
absorbing the weak New Mexico spring—
it's OK to shuffle for a while
with the agnostics because the white-
faced Death who tinkles

a soft bell ahead of Jesus
calls everyone to step in the walk
past embarrassments of booth-sweets & tourist
rosaries: this Death
for whom maracas knock

wears plastic huaraches under his muslin
shroud spotted with candle-wax.
Then, finally, the four enter in robes, swaying
with the advertised Cristo

Crucificado, red & grainy piñon,
borne on 2 × 4s, the wool of his knitted scalp
catching on splinters.
I'm by the entrance
to belief where cripples groan

deeper into whatever genetic
twist to kiss a photographed Jesus—
see across the placard their wet kisses

step, bleaching details
from God's face. They carry a Jesus so heavy
that their knees buckle in the dance—
their art is grief
so complex in its steps that the young
falter & the old go down

thrashing in the telepathic spill.
If not one of us is healthy,
yet we try to sing,
as those to whom I'm joined now
hand to hand sing against my mental defect

that won't let me roll
as the uniformed Daughters of the Sacrament
roll, their capes sluicing on the tile floor.

Driving with One Light

that strokes shapes out of the trees,
that makes far-back animal eyes
prickle, I fight right
then left the two halves of an S-curve

four hours into the Sierras.
I keep the white
centerline flowing under the VW,
denying the peripheral

animal world that flares momentarily.
I'm in a second world
the radio makes because sleep presumes

that first world I will not to enter.
Wrong-facing signs reflect my only light
as the two-lane road overtakes

rockface turn, then tree then tree.
In the righthand dark something lives,
spreads against the windshield,

then breaks through
to where I am, civilized, wary & cursing.
I flap my arms as the creature flaps

in the glass shards.
Tree patterns come into the light,
then trees as the car skids,
parting laurel & low brush

I oddly try to name
before the car stops, tearing a visible blaze
in a big Doug fir.
Whatever it is is across one leg

as I roll out the sprung door;
it moves, it flutters as I push
my back against the door,
trapping inside the worst I can imagine—

nothing so simple as a feathered self,
nothing so arcane you couldn't make it out,
least light, in you.

PART II
FICTIONS

Halloween

But the costumes won't come off—
beast face,
or the skeletal kid whose mom lipsticked

on his pimpled midriff
a working stomach
& lungs so real he had to hold his breath

twice not to inhale
pee-marks & the dumpster smell
through alley shortcuts

& past hard-hat bars.
Now you sidle past pimps' Rivieras
& pink LTDs, animal life

barely cool in the animal
skin seats the got-up girls warm
as they echo in fatigued mews

the long riff of cat-scream
gaudy love
could blare when you're caught

in the body wild to lay down
your muzzle,
your hair on end, witless,

against another pelt.
Out of the neighborhood,
middle-class porchlights blue

the jungle dark.
Go in through the hinged dog-door,
pawing a grip on linoleum to lie

where Lawrence Welk or
Honeymooners reruns soothe some grandma
or widower grandpa lonely &

moaning with the Welk brass section.
This is how you learn *human*
until the ends of the lyric tangle

in your long ears,
& the TV is off, the picture pinched
down to a dot.

Then pad haltingly after the halting
other you'll replace as he or she limps—
like you soloing on hind legs,

not quite human still, but trying, trying.

Chicago: State & Van Buren

Puppet-woman pulled to tiptoe
sings gospel
in a man's counterfeited voice.
It's almost dusk,
but you can see sneakers down

under the cloth backdrop; you can see
strings let down through sky-holes
twitch her into an alto

"How Great Thou Art."
Loop theaters wink out of the Chicago collage
the street guy named Apostle
pasted behind his box-sized stage—
minute world, the focus

concentrates desire not belief.
A tired clerk turns off the power
in Goldblatt's southwest window

behind Apostle & begins to undress
a dummy, first
skinning off the checked skirt.

The Apparatus

The two-stroke pump stutters at
a manhole
opening: rancid, the first blister

of stuff in the gutter,
first gauzy spurt
from the pipe-end. Cabrini
Project kids bail it back

with their hands,
soak up shirtsful.
One, the linguist, who sticks his head
down the hole, catches

hair-ends in the apparatus & grunts.
He sees a soup
of arms & legs shadowy below
fluttering at the suction

of the feed-in,
but what charms him
is the noise he wants

to talk to—
the Capone guns & a modern
skag-boosted syncopation—
a music the others begin

to hear,
the diminuendo gold slaver
burbling out against their sneakers.
The apparatus changes pitch;
they hammer at it

with rocks & a taped fungo bat.
They bloody knuckles & curse, beating
until it stalls, swallows its own
music with the discharge.

The Pour

Four of us men by twos lug
the 20-gallon
meltdown kettles in step
with the glowing

kettle ahead,
our company coveralls
flowering spills
& then burn marks,

our heavy shoes crusted
with sugar magma we'll pour
smoking in the cold
spread-room

where the "spread" girls
choir sweet
damns, greased gloves up
as they back for us

tight to the walls
("peanut-brittle"
was Nov. when "mayonnaise"
shut down).

I prayed after twenty
carries for flu,
my forearms twitching,
prayed all night

as I steered
the bulky kettle to the tables
with my partner's body.
God talked

to me in the toilet
about the girls,
the old one who spits
into the sizzle before

she calls it names
of her man whose knob
she wants burned
off before she ends her shift.

But I urge & I urge God
for the flat-nose girl
with the sugar blister
in the V of her uniform

she shows as she bends,
devoted, to the pour.

Climbing Sears Tower

*"Stuntman Daniel Goodwin, dressed in a
Spiderman outfit, climbs west face of building,
using suction cups and metal devices, in 7½
hours . . . is arrested after ascending the 1,454 foot
building."—New York Times,* 5/26/81

4 hours into the climb,
you're still in a reflected Chicago,
against the reflected downtown
grid of older buildings, hardly discernible

humans mirrored close
to your cheek on the breath-wet glass.
Or maybe you imagine humans,
imagine their small concerns

after some time trying.
The sky comes
onto the glass some floors later;
it includes a TV copter

you don't turn to see
examining you, wanting the arachnid
change TV will show as pathos.
You sweat across a divided sun

into the out-of-focus
western neighborhoods where I imagine
the Douglas el rattling
past my window on Leavitt, sucking

curtain against the rusted screen —
instead, the copter camera
shows fatigue-points a wiseass announcer
superimposes on your back

as though you're holding Humboldt Park
like a bandage over racial turmoil.
He looks for human
failure, for regret not exhaustion —

as the bartender switches to the Cubs
& miming a spider scurry,
clears lunch glasses, olives & chorizo

scraps into a basin.

Sterno

squeezed, rag-strained for the waxy
alcohol,
sipped for mortal fire:
the coatless man drinks it,
tasting equally rapture

& *a priori* death,
his few teeth coating & his breath,
when he swallows it,
burning down to mere appetite

for more breath.
Crying out, having put his tongue to it,
he is immune
like the literalist porcupine

at last free to eat the toad
he's surprised himself by catching,
devouring first the toad's poison

gland, lathering his face toxic.
The man thrashes
the wet municipal lawn, rolls
against a camphor tree
the rain has thrashed into perfumed

wakefulness, coating
but not diluting his man-smell
for the park cop who hunkers
over him, a nightstick's length away,
his leather cop-harness creaking

as he flicks snails
off the sweet creases in the man's face.

Zoo

In its envy, the white-bibbed okapi tramples
the peacock—over the clay
the stutter of its hooves, all expletives.
That's why the boy is let go

by moonlight, charms glued to his chest,
into the grass-eaters-of-the-African-veldt corral.
Naked, savage for their cure,
he scares a pygmy oribi that's clearing mimosa

rubbish from the watering trough
with its muzzle.
As it runs, khaki then
umber in the little light, it coughs
& coughs feathery mimosa

blossoms; the boy won't go after, but in turn
drinks out of the trough
clogged mouthsful. Slowly, then, he tracks

in the tracks, his feet tender,
past the padlocked feed bins where a one-bulb
glow makes straw a brocade.
He'll let the stopped antelope sniff,

let it lick mimosa drool
from his lips as he tries to assimilate
through each link in the food chain

empty anger that like sex
is the ache for absent parts the other has.
Another night he'll cure

the lazy meat-eaters, stand
for man, in thought's brothel find his ecstasy,
so afraid urine drops muddy
on his leg, his ribs clawed with his own hands.
He'll let them nip him,

let fang or claw drag
the hairless interstices of his body.
Only those trapped between the literal

& an appetite—these he can't help:
the greedy mouse a whole week caught in poultry wire
goes on growing, one half *head,*
the other half *rosy-anus-in-fur-threads* —
the wire opening closed on its middle,
it eats in the emu's pen & defecates

in freedom.

Halloween Creature

with Spock ears & a snout
incongruously mixed, & the other child his mother
& I pretend not to know,
who came home as a tree, bark lapped on

like feathers—both their bodies
are so closely zipped,
buttoned, or sewn into the bizarre

that the bodies can't fall apart
in sleep. The younger one's in bed
with inked-on leaf veins still crawling
his hands as I talk

from his brother's bed opposite:
it is Oct. 31 everywhere
& there are no children because
we must do what the costumes tell us—
adults must live

to extinction in Jordache or Izod casuals
while kids have feathers or fur,
& they eat the meat-threaded wind

from burger-stands,
cursed with an appetite for grass.
To tell my sons more, I must make the '40s
Riverview Park & around it nighttime
Chicago, literal but dissolving in neon lather:
we're on the 80 ft. hump

one's head takes before the stomach follows
Dead Man's Curve
& the roller-coaster cars dive
again into gravity.
You hear screams best under the structure,

your forehead against a cool girder,
your bladder tight with Orange Crush or beer,
believing in alone
though there must be a dozen other pissers
in the dark around you, & that colicky moan

each gives dopplers to a metal-on-metal
group screech as the train passes,
& in the overhead bars of light
you see paint flecks
snowing: the structure bearing up all the orbits

shivers but stays.
Ignore all this, the Parachute Jump,
Giant Wheel, but be drawn in your listening
to the carousel where animals
once danced their limited steps around

a march tune's 3-minute circuit,
& now you see only humans
on poles prancing for their riders
the intricate human round

of gestures — you must ride them,
selecting your parents by what you want to be,
riding, your furry thighs
tightening at the percussion parts

of the song, your hearts accelerating
until you sleep.

PART III

The Grand Egress

was Barnum's way to stir
believers, usher them out before they gave way
facing the wolf-faced boy
along the clogged path to the next tent,

their dimes already gone & the boy growling
what could be words.
TO THE GRAND EGRESS Barnum's sign with an arrow
said, as though some fresh

atrocity, on its haunches, waited.
So believers left the boy's world before grief
at the differences between them
overcame joy at their likeness.
My brother's joy was to guide me

past dangers, the detours child-logic
cuts through fences
the long way to school, Iowa snow painting out
unpaved walks, even the ERIE RAILROAD & SOO LINE
escutcheons on the boxcar sides
of the 75-car freight stopped as far as

our wheel-level eyes could look.
& snow melting on the still-hot tracks.
Trains could be on the spur
past class-bell sometimes, past our short legs'
strength, wavering, as Joseph Campbell says,

before the absolute.
Religions, he goes on, make the way to dying
grand as Barnum's exit come-on
so that no one would linger here

loving the animal, capitulating.
Gerry & I blocked by a long freight,
breath-beards condensing on our mufflers.
Stooping, we saw snow on that side

as on this, & old footprints.
Dirty ice hanging from the couplings
& behind the wheels,
studded with gravel & cinders the wheels threw.
It won't move, Gerry said, scrambling,

gratuitously dropping a book, bending again
under the wheel for it.
From the other side, he leaned & looked
across at me, looked, not a boy at all.
Hell, I wanted to go under,
I still want to go under.

Instructions for Rowing

across the reflected sun the skiff cuts
should include diagrams
of the radius joint of the wrist,
a kind of human oarlock.
The island in his head the sweated rower looks at

is sublime in a way
the island one can't face to row to never is:
so deliberately choose a distant

mark to go away from—
this is the way to go straight

to what you can't face. Your father's distant
cousin drowned rehearsing suicide,
& the fish you think of eat

under his clothes
(your wrists ache already)—
but this is your *mother's* cousin's island.
The scoured paint-cans

for berrying & your brother's little weight
hold all this in balance.
& balance is somewhere in the ear
a fish doesn't have.
The water which substitutes for thought

runs inaudible through the fish.
It senses its world full-length:
its balance is the dark nerve-matter along its spine
aligned to the imagined horizon.
How different a boy is

consuming father's cousin in a joke
to scare younger brother,
who wails & won't look into the muddy swirl.

Pause when no current corrects the skiff.
You are there
when willow roots tangle your oars;
the back of your head will brush through the trailing

branches the inside of your head saw.

Matthew's Lesson

fails, yet the piano learns the music
a 10-year-old wants
to make: this difficult June

the fingers pace into,
counting rhythm with the heart or breath—
I hear it through the roses

that I weed outside his practice room.
Separating the bermuda
grass's successive, fugal nettings
from rose thorns,
my fingers inattentively rub
pain as his rub song—I have blood-dots

on my wrists & dirt
from which I take blood-smell.
The music stops
as my fingers find the roots,

the earth pulling back
at my pull. Matthew, I know, is listening
for what I hear as I listen,
as quiet as I can be

to the process the Bach exercise
posits because silence
is a challenge, not an evasion, the musician
dares—each of us listens

on his side of the open window.

41

Catfishing

  is best hot July midnights,
stars catching on a ragged
horizon the willow-lined slough makes,

the Coleman light
coloring nearby berry canes green.
The crawfish traps dry out,
crawfish pieces
still crusted to the wire netting

crawfish consciousness fought through—
what can a 12-year-old know,
what do I teach
in teaching Paul to crack them
& pull the hook-barb against

the snarled little flesh & leave them
living to go again over
the uneven slough floor?
Catfish eat anything

with a hard-lipped smile—
Paul should learn all
I don't want to teach him,
should imagine crawfish pain & the steel

in him teaching him sideways
moves in the ooze he can't imagine
until I show him how
to handmold the local favorite
bait: deliberately dirtied blood

& meal, the chicken guts
three days in a jar.
Mosquitoes knot along his arm;
he twitches the rod,
properly hoping to catch nothing.

Blue

Reroofing first our shed's south,
weather-burned slant,
I lever up by pairs the crumbly cedar shakes,

the sun that's annealed to the roofing nails,
while I breathe in rot,
insect casings & incidental dirt

that puffs black under my pry.
On my knees, I dance back from vertigo
until for balance I must put my eye

down to the splintery hole
I've accidentally broken, & with that one eye
drop through shelves, tool clips,

& so many coffee cans of nails
that they rust
what light the hole draws down.

I'm dizzy but resist memory that tastes,
thing by thing, love's famine.
When I pull my eye back from the hole,

the things by their gravity stay
the absolutes our family kept
negotiating: against Fran's temper,

put her immutable black-sheep status;
for the X-mas cards
trussed but never sent (1968),

give shelves of home-canned cukes going
green a second time.
I bob & twist to look away,

slivers cross-stitched into my knees
& up the gloves I slap
& paw through, compensating—

I hang on at last only by looking away,
only by relacing with my eye
the garage wall's clematis against

the down-there—by eye hanging, for example,
the drying laundry, sock to contiguous
shirt to shirt, concentrating

every way I can to make fit the last piece,
our tied-back puppy who on two legs
nips the Levi's hung crotch up: blue

flows out of the sky into them.

The Spider

All a March week I watch,
stopping the fretsaw,
spilling brads & the birdhouse

pegs, watching the spider
caress a braille of light-dots,
no-weight angles
of the victim-eater paradigm

I deny as I too build, my hands
all encysted slivers & hammer-bruises,
for song the finches repeat

to their images, the counter-birds,
in the garage-shop windows
they fly at, tapping, turning aside
from death only by looking to the trees.

But my look won't lift,
& my song is to myself as the very small

birdhouse hole tightens around me.
Each day the sun slides
later on the window toward a web

more comprehensive.
So I sand the grainless pine parts, align jig
for glue & the pin-small brads,

relishing each task,
even indecorously eating at the bench,
wanting to finish when the spider does.

Ladder

Head at sill-level,
she looks back into her bedroom,
out of reach: her school clothes,
the plump Hummel kids,
the posters bellying out from moist

August walls.
The outside stucco rasps
her toes, rasps knuckles
she thinks are big
when the chain fire-ladder
sways & she goes down by feel

into adult illusion,
to watch her parents in their window
kiss TV kisses past the 10 P.M. news,

sleep into the late show she's denied.
Her fingers numb in the flow of chain.
Neighbors' lights ripple
up her pj's as she comes legs first

down into the yellow & mistuned taupe
that flares around the actors.
If she could lean through
the window's initial cool to that
burning they pretend

to endure, she'd speckle
with love-sweat too.
Now she noseprints the glass;

she's twisted up in ladder,
aching all over
to lip-synch a love she can't yet hear.
She doesn't know the sound

is off; her mother has let go
her sleeping father's hand—
each of them is adrift
in real life so prolix with echoes
that suffering
blazes out of each word love could say.

La Traviata

In the drafty Kiwanis hall
still hung with V–E Day bunting,
my mother, your sister, pounded out
"Addio, del passato" for you, Violetta-

dying-to-manipulative-love.
The senior judge, a voice coach, grunted
& shifted in his folding chair
as you lifted your hands to the fleur-de-lys

stamped metal ceiling,
crying inadequately but believing yourself.
Five rows back, I must've looked
up, Violetta, from my Marvel

comic, thinking myself that Marvel hero
so wounded that medicos had condemned each
of his bodily processes separately—
inside his mask a face so hideous,

so amorphous from the lab accident
that only the mask held it together
(each spangle an actual bolt-head),

the blue mask hiding blue skin—
like you a victim,
not a weak Alfredo I couldn't understand.
In the front row, three other Violettas,

their heads worked in duplicate
nineteen-forties' finger-curls,
turned as I suddenly coughed

& bled on the comic pages.
Even my occult ability to constrict the atoms
of my body at will couldn't stop

a simple nosebleed.
After the audition my mother raged —
but who is to say we two had no right

to try to suffer, to grow into detail,
sotto voce imitate better singers
dying, each pretending so hard
that the notes come out bloodstained,
though not song.

So High

that you can see where you fell
from the Dunkerton silo
    at nine, or the sumac spear
I aimed at you,
threatening your eye—the retrospect
    is all the way

to childhood—you're riding the sway,
each foot cupped
    in last year's scions,
sawing, sawing a place for the sun

to freckle onto the roses.
    My role is brake
on the nylon line I've tied to my waist,
a Möbius-twist that loops

yellow through the camphor
    tree's eternal green. Bark comes down;
then you scab off a bootheel
    like some body part,
always pulling more line until I lose
what I knew of you.
    One tree's enough

logic to climb through imagining
    veer under the elbowdeep green,
taking countless
false handholds until you come out

in sky. Now the sun multiplies
      off your tools,
but you won't ripple the saw again
      through the steady groan

of the wood—you've seen the horizon
      cut by roof-peaks
in your balkanized neighborhood of small lots.
      In identical trees you see
other men sway
      over reflected heat thrown
up from the asphalt shingles: you wave

they wave.

for my brother, Gerry

Eden

*"I am very young & ye are very old
wherefore I was afraid."* —Job, XII

Sprinklers spot the patio
edges, spot the rest-home piano which gives
us Scarlatti or '40s

show tunes but means heaven is not denied
even the reluctant,
those so old they'll have to die twice.
As my wife goes on playing,
seedpods smack
& flatten out under chair-wheels:

around us is a garden
so choked & many-minded that size
is a function
of reconciled disregard.
Ebullient suckers twig out after

ten feet of desperate trying,
their leaves half-clenched
but green. Behind poked-out screens,

inside the rest home,
something even older hums
back—replete, unanimous in the music
my wife uses to call them:

burr-faced grandpas
so inward they are almost amoebic,
the grandmas in lumps under sheets—
the bed-restrained

who are already marked
into zones by straps begin to divide,
loins sinking toward buttocks,
cleft toward cleft until
the first tear is made into two humans—
the one who wants to die

& the left half that will draw all the organs
into altered gravity.
This Saturday I help the muscular nurse

push chairs,
against the rules go in where she does,
wanting to understand

graffiti that says "don't look for me"
or "God took my children first,"
wanting at last their wanting,
wanting to bring them all back
for whom we sang.

Made in the USA
Middletown, DE
11 January 2017

3932331R00089

WITHDRAWN
No longer the property of the
Boston Public Library.
Sale of this material benefits the Library

IT IS HERE. IT IS DANGEROUS.

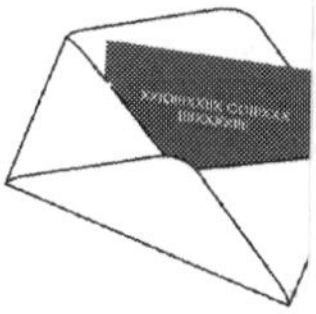

Sale of this mat... ...ents the Library.

No longer the property of the ... ston ... Library.

WITHDRAWN

THE FUTURE
of EMAIL

WHAT WE MUST DO
TO PROTECT OURSELVES

V.A. SHIVA PhD

THE INVENTOR OF EMAIL

Dr. V. A. Shiva

To Freedom

© 2016. V.A. Shiva Ayyadurai.

All rights reserved. No part of this publication may be reproduced, distributed, or transmitted in any form or by any means, including photocopying, recording, or other electronic or mechanical methods, without the prior written permission of the publisher, except in the case of brief quotations embodied in critical reviews and certain other noncommercial uses permitted by copyright law.

Printed in the United States of America.

First Edition, 2016.

ISBN 978-0-9970402-3-4

General Interactive, LLC
Publishing Division
701 Concord Ave.
Cambridge, MA 02138
www.generalinteractive.com

All proceeds from the sale of this book go to Innovation Corps, a 501 (c) not-for-profit project.
www.innovation-corps.org

CONTENTS

9

Author's Note

Email, the system I invented in 1978, while a 14-year-old boy, to enable collaboration and communication among office workers at a small medical college in Newark, NJ, has now become the center of many controversies. For their 125th Anniversary issue, *The Wall Street Journal* commissioned me as email's inventor to write a brief essay entitled *The Future of Email*. That article shared what email really is and where email is heading. More recently, *The New York Times* interviewed me to comment on Hillary Clinton's use of personal email server to manage classified U.S. government communications. In that article, I shared that the use of a personal email server was extraordinary, wrong and clearly a well-planned strategy by Ms. Clinton to deny the American public's rightful access to communications that were government property.

This book is a much-needed expansion of those thoughts and comments to provide you important insights to where email is going and why you as citizens must take action to protect this important medium, which has been subverted by vested interests. I believe with all sincerity and without hyperbole you should listen to what I'm going to share, as I am not only the world's leading expert on this subject but also have a historical and political perspective that will enable you to realize that if we do not act, our freedom, which has already been compromised, will suffer even more greatly, in a future where Have's and Have Not's will be defined by the level of security they have to their email communications.

I hope this book provides you the information you need and deserve to make the right decisions.

V. A. SHIVA
Cambridge, MA

8

INTRODUCTION

Wake Up

"The more it changes, the more it's the same."

This phrase ("Plus ça change, plus c'est la même chose") first appeared in a French literary journal in 1849. The phrase is worth thinking about in the context of our present day environment, where we tend to focus on the enormous changes and innovations that have taken place in the past few decades, especially in the role of technology in our everyday lives. I would be the last one to deny those awesome changes, and this book intends to look closely at exactly how they work and what they will mean.

But let's look first at a few things that have not changed, at least since human beings stopped hunting wooly mammoths with sticks and stones and societies started to organize themselves.

The ancient Greeks and Romans, the Aztecs of pre-Columbian Mexico, the Mongols of central Asia, the European monarchies of the Middle Ages – wherever

9

you look in human history, societies have been organized into "elites" and "everybody else." The elites have always ruled, and they're still ruling.

Qualification for membership in an elite have changed and varied over the centuries. It was not always gender-based. Early on, matriarchies were common. Later, military prowess skewed rulership toward males. Priesthoods also developed. Supposed connections with gods and goddesses conferred major benefits right here on Earth.

The United States, technically speaking, is a representative democracy: "One nation, under God, indivisible, with liberty and justice for all." That's a beautiful foundation for a country, or at least an aspiration. But really the US is ruled by its own version of elites, and oligarchs rule. As that French maxim suggests, the details have changed but the basic system remains intact.

I've chosen that word "system" very deliberately. I am a systems scientist, with four degrees from MIT. I've studied systems theory at the intersection of technology, medicine, and artificial intelligence for many years. I've learned that all systems, including political ones, depend on just two essential properties.

The first property is *observability* -- the capacity to watch the operation of the system in detail, to recognize its trajectory, and ideally to measure the input and output of the system at any point in time.

The second property is *predictability* -- the ability to regulate the inputs of a

10

system in order to obtain an expected and desired output.

For any system, therefore, whether it's a machine or a garden or a whole society, observability and predictability are the basis of control. Whoever wishes to control a system must know, or observe, exactly what the current inputs and outputs of the system are, and must then have the ability to manipulate the system's inputs in order to generate predictable output.

By itself, none of this is inherently good or bad. In the system of your own life, for example, observability and predictability are thoroughly positive when used for setting goals that can advance you creatively, emotionally, intellectually, and even financially.

Technology can be hugely beneficial toward achieving those goals. Technology can be a powerful tool for enabling each of us to connect with and express our innate and unique gifts as individual human beings. But technology can also take us in negative and destructive directions, especially when it's controlled not by ourselves but by a distant, manipulative elite.

Instead of enhancing our ability to express ourselves as individuals, technology can literally transform us into something much closer to a machine --- an automaton or mindless robot. Right now, that might seem like an extreme statement, but by the end of this book you'll have a fuller understanding of what it means, and you'll see how true it really is.

The specific concern of the book will be the past, present, and future of email -- the communications system I invented at the age of fourteen in 1978, and

which is now used by billions of people every day to send trillions of messages every year. But focusing on email can be enlightening not just because its use is so widespread. Certain essential features of email – we'll discuss them in the chapters that follow – make email intensely personal in spite of (or because of) the seemingly impersonal nature of the technology itself.

For most people, email is written and read quickly and spontaneously. It's closer to the process of human thought than earlier forms of communication. Email can be deceptively intimate but also (unbeknownst to most people) deceptively *public* as well. Consequently, the future of email contains both opportunity and danger, and one of my primary intentions for this book is to clarify both the possibilities and the perils.

In the relatively short lifespan of email so far, there have already been declarations that email is "dead." Usually this death of email is linked to its supposed replacement by text messaging and social media in one form or another. I am certain, however, that the use of email in new and creative ways remains wide open. We have only scratched the surface.

There are many reasons why email is and will remain a dynamically growing and essential medium. Because the death of email has been so persistently written about, I want to cite a number of reasons why email is very much alive.

>> Email facilitates engaging and rich communication. It is not limited to the few hundred characters imposed by text message systems. Content, presentation, and creativity make email a substantial and

flexible platform for both personal and business communication.

>> Email IS controllable. Email is the ideal medium in situations that require control of information that is transmitted to recipients. The amount of information that is sent to each recipient can be directed by the sender, in contrast to social media platforms in which such controls are absent or unwieldy. Since email is asynchronous, sender can control when they want to send and receive email -- unlike social media or text messaging, which are generally instantaneous.

>> Email can be personalized to the receiving individual or group. This is not possible with social media platforms, through which everyone reads the same information.

>> Email has been legally validated. Since email is a written form of communication, courts have ruled that email is a legal and enforceable document of record. On the other hand, social media postings and text messaging are not considered to be legally admissible records, except in some special cases.

>> Email continues to be the best option for permission-based reach. It can be used both for single opt-in and double opt-in methods of subscription or news dissemination. Social media are not capable of this.

>> Email is familiar and easy to use. With constant refinement of the technology, email easily passes the

"Mom and Pop Usability Test," unlike social media and messaging which are less user-friendly.

>> Email has evolved over the years and is now extremely stable, and reliable. Standards and technologies for email transmission and retrieval have become universal, and implementing email is easy compared with the complexity of XML- and RSS-based social media systems which are still not standardized.

>> Email is universally accessible. Email can be accessed on any communications platform, from the latest tech gadgets and the newest smart phones to much older models.

>> Email is an ideal "push medium." Email is well-adapted for pushing information or data to recipients, unlike social media which is more pull oriented. This is of great advantage when you there is a limited opportunity to grab a reader's attention.

>> Email will live as long as businesses will live. Email is the communications tool of choice for businesses today. Social media and text messaging are useful for short exchanges, but are ill suited for business communication where typically a larger amount of data has to be moved, and archiving of communications is required.

I hope what you've read so far has enhanced your understanding of this technology, and has clarified how email has really changed the world. But we must view all

this in the context of the enduring historical reality that I mentioned earlier. Remember: human societies are organized as "in" groups and "out groups," elites and non-elites. As a systems scientist, I can assure you this is how the human system works.

The elites who rule us now have done whatever they can to co-opt the email that I invented in 1978, ironically using the foundations of a technology called EchoMail that I also created, in 1993. EchoMail utilizes artificial intelligence to analyze the content of incoming email, even in very large volumes, and then to respond by again using AI.

For the elites, the short-term purpose of this is to make money from you. More to the point, the purpose is to make as much money as possible from you – to literally turn you into a money-dispensing machine, a robotic ATM. Most distressing of all, you might already be one, because email – which you probably use every day – is probably the most powerful means ever created for enabling this drone-conversion to take place.

But that's not the end of the story. You can make the choice to change the system that surrounds you by learning about the technology that empowers it. In particular, I want to show how email is the foundational technology that enables businesses, and also the government, to have a direct and powerful influence on people's lives. I want to show how email accomplishes this not only by what is transmitted to the private citizens, but also through careful analysis and use of what those citizens transmit themselves.

The emails that are sent, the emails that are received, and the devices (the machines) that send and receive

them are transforming our environment – and also transforming us in very literal ways. They are changing us physically, emotionally, and psychologically. They have already changed us much more than most people realize. Even Karl Marx, in his seminal work *Das Kapital*, could not foresee the effects of such machines, which he thought would ultimately free us from labor, integral to the creation of a communist society.

Marx believed that industrial workers would bring about revolutionary change. These workers, who found themselves victimized by the mills and factories of the industrial revolution, and who were compelled to work for the lowest possible wages in order to create surplus value for the capitalist owners, were destined to rise up. Angry and alienated from their work and their lives in general, they would turn their backs on their machines, take to the streets, and create a revolution to bring about the next momentous stage of human history, the "dictatorship of the proletariat."

In *The Communist Manifesto* (1848), Marx and Friedrich Engels described this process in some detail. There were reasons why it was necessary for national authority to be seized and administered by the industrial workers:

> "The first step on the path to the workers' revolution is the elevation of the proletariat to the position of ruling class. The proletariat will gain from its political domination by gradually tearing away from the bourgeoisie all capital, by centralizing all means of production in the hands of the State, that is, in the hands of the

proletariat itself organized as the ruling class."

In later writings, Marx theorized about the dictatorship of the proletariat as a transitional period between the exploitative, destructive environment of capitalist society and the idealized, totally fulfilling communist society that would come later. Capitalism was the dictatorship of the factory owners and landowners. It would be replaced by the socialist dictatorship of the proletariat, which would, eventually, becomes a classless, stateless society – a kind of heaven on earth.

But Marx never really described what the dictatorship of the proletariat would actually look like, and he certainly never described the new Garden of Eden that was supposed to come next. He did allude to the use of machines to alleviate humans from the drudgery of menial work. It's easy to imagine an action movie of the industrial workers rushing out of their factories, but it's more difficult to imagine them actually administrating a highly developed society.

But none of this happened anyway. Nothing even remotely like it happened. What did happen has been well documented, both in print and in blood, and I will not revisit it here. Instead, I will offer my own glimpse into the future, which, like that of Marx, concerns machines, mankind, and revolution – but in ways that Marx never imagined. Neither did anyone else, of course, and most people still can't imagine it. But here it comes anyway.

It will surprise no one that the machines I have in mind are not the tool and die makers, the extruders, or the blast furnaces of old. Cellphones, laptops, and tablets are what I'm thinking of – the instruments, themselves, the tasks they perform, and the revolutionary changes they are about to foment.

"But," you might say, "haven't they already fomented those changes. Why, look how I can send instant messages to my brother-in-law in Seattle, or even talk to him on Skype." And I say, "That's nothing. That's nothing compared to what's coming, and coming very soon."

The way things are actually turning out is an interesting spin on what Marx thought was going to happen. Marx was correct to recognize that the interaction between man and machine was going to be the source of fundamental change. But he was wrong about how it would start happening or how the change would continue.

Marx painted an imaginary picture of enraged workers storming out of their factories, leaving their machines behind. They were furious with their machines. They couldn't wait to get away from them. Perhaps they would even destroy the machines before racing out into the streets.

That dramatic scenario is just the opposite of what's actually taking place. Today, instead of running away from their machines, people are getting closer and closer to their machines all the time. But, needless to say, the machines I'm referring to aren't the iron hulks of the old days. Thanks to Bill Gates, the machines have operating systems that make them more efficient than any flesh

and blood human assistant. Thanks to Steve Jobs, the new machines are lightweight, stylish, portable, smooth to the touch, and even affectionate in their way. When people say – as they often do – "I couldn't live without my iPhone," that may be a hyperbole at the present moment. But just wait.

Now let's go even further. Instead of separating from their machines as Marx predicted, and instead of even becoming very close to their machines or feeling that their machines are indispensable, people will *become one with their machines* -- and I mean that literally. The line between "you" and "it" is going to disappear completely. That line is already getting very blurred.

When that line is gone, you won't feel very differently. You'll just feel *more* of the way you feel now. As mentioned earlier, you already feel like you "can't live without" your iPhone. In the future -- the near future -- something like that will be literally true, except the distinction between you and the device will have effectively disappeared – so "I can't live without" will be a meaningless statement.

In writing about these issues, it's difficult to break free of a "human-centric" point of view. After all, people have been Earth's dominant life form for some time now. We tend to think that will continue, even if some re-calibration may take place. But what I see coming down the tracks is more than a re-calibration.

Is it more like a replacement?

My work with email is what really opened my mind to all this. As it became possible to create automated emails that seemed like someone – not a machine – had actually sat down and written them, this question of

19

course arose: could you tell whether you were communicating with a person or a machine?

Now, I believe, some even more startling questions need to be answered: are you a machine, or are you becoming a machine? Where does "you" stop, and "machine" begin?

Here is the danger. The more we become machines, (or already are), *without being aware of it*, the easier it is to observe and control us. It may be valuable to become cyborgs, on some level --- better eyesight, better levels of perception, etc. but if we are not aware that we are becoming machines, therein is the danger. Today, those in power meticulously and creatively control us as machines by manipulating what email content we receive using AI and "Big Data." They observe our thoughts, which are directly embedded in those emails, en masse, to predict and manipulate the trajectory of our behavior.

Their goal of is to make you into an unconscious machine, a robot, because then you become more observable and more predictable. The evolution of email provides an incredible opportunity to witness how this drone-conversion is taking place. This book will wake you up and inspire you to make conscious choices --- perhaps even compel you to demand broader changes to regain the freedom that makes us human.

You will learn the true promise of email --- its original intention and, how the advent of "free" email services now enable governments and large corporations to make us far more OBSERVABLE. You will learn from my work as an "insider" with President Clinton's White House and with some of largest Fortune 1000 brands, who deployed AI technology such as EchoMail,

how email is being used to make you more PREDICTABLE.

So, there is a revolution all right, the elites want to control you by making you more and more observable and predictable. Email is their medium of choice for this control. In parallel, technological advances are making you one with the machines of human creation. You have a choice to embrace this evolution, with awareness and wake up, so you do not give up your freedom.

Since you have chosen to read this book, you've likely made a decision to fight for it.

PART 1

The Promise

CHAPTER 1

The Evolution of the Digital World

Billions of email messages are sent every day. Each email message is the written word. It contains our private thoughts, be they intimate, formal, legal or financial to one or many. However, the written word was not always the medium for such communication.

Before the widespread use of written language, stories and myths were shared orally and were preserved through repetition, often by large groups of people in collaborative performances. This was true of the *Mahabharata* and the *Ramayana*, the great epics of India, as well as the *Illiad* and the *Odyssey* in ancient Greece.

The development of written language and technical innovations – everything from papyrus to the printing press – made long-term and long-range communication possible. This was particularly valuable for administration and commerce, as well as for literature and even entertainment. In fact, literally every form of communication and media in the modern world has

developed from our ability to convey information across space and time.

But the defining characteristics of these media are very different. In the world of handwritten messages, a sticky note (the brand name Post-It), a community bulletin board, and a hard copy paper letter serve unique purposes that are clearly differentiated. Exploration of their properties can reveal the underlying assumptions and cultural effects in the modern world of both print and digital text-based communications leading to a *relational and accurate* understanding of what email really is. Currently confusing definitions of email as "electronic messaging" or "text messaging" exist on popular sites such as *Wikipedia*.

To overcome this, it's best to understand email by its relationship to other media. This should include a contextual and historical analysis of various kinds of communication, beginning with the earliest forms and continuing into the digital era.

This understanding requires a "space" in which to explore the nature of email relative to other media. We define that relational space by proposing three independent forms of communication in the contemporary world:

- Short Messaging
- Community Messaging
- Intimate (or Formal) Messaging

These three modes of messaging appear to be invariant across both print and digital media. They have

analogs in historical forms of communication, as indicated in the chart below.

The Three Forms of Messaging

	Pre-modern	Print Era	Electronic & Digital Era
Short Messaging	Smoke Signal	Sticky Note	Telegram, Text message, Tweet,
Community Messaging	Cave Painting	Bulletin Board, Graffiti	Discussion boards, Blogs, Facebook
Intimate (or Formal) Messaging	Clay Tablet, Papyrus	Letter and Memo	Email message

Each mode of messaging serves very different purposes. Short messaging condenses a lot of information into a small amount of space and is valuable for rapid and efficient communication. I remember in the "old days" receiving a telegram from my relative in India: "YOUR BELOVED UNCLE HAS PASSED ON." Given the limitation of space and the cost per character, the writer had no choice but to be brief. Today, when one sends tweets, the adage "brevity is the soul of wit," becomes more important than ever.

On the other hand, community messaging is for open, transparent and public participation where interactions enable sharing of a common story or

provide a forum for open dialog and debate. In prehistoric times, after a hunt, a clan would draw paintings using plant dyes on cave walls. The cave wall was their "facebook." Graffiti on public walls in modern times is an extension of the human desire for such communal communication.

The bulletin board, in public hallways of high schools, on telephone poles, and at shop retailers, provides a way for community "postings," advertisements and comments using paper and pins. In the electronic and digital era, community messaging reappears in blogs, Facebook, Pinterest, LinkedIn, etc. where now millions participate in discussions, debates and share opinions on electronic "walls."

Unlike short messaging and community messaging, however, intimate messaging is typically for longer or more formal communication, either one to one, or one to many, where privacy is critical. In ancient times, clay tablets and papyrus were used to record major speeches, essays, love letters, legal contracts and financial transactions. The Rosetta Stone being one of the stellar examples of this.

The advent of the printed letter and typewritten memos extended the reach of such communication across time and space through interoffice mail systems in business environments and through postal systems across the world. Email emerged from the extension of this lineage of interoffice and postal communications.

There are two other important observations from the chart above. First, each form of messaging uses different media. Short messaging uses media such as

smoke signals, sticky notes, telegrams, tweets and text messages.

Second, each medium *does not exist* independent of the *system* necessary to support the medium. Before the invention of a particular system, the particular form of messaging itself does not exist. For example, people for thousands of years were burning wood and generating smoke. But it took some clever person to come up with an entire system of using that smoke to create a *smoke signal* and method of communicating using smoke.

Only when inventors create the particular communication system does the medium of that messaging system emerge. There could be no telegram had Samuel Morse not interconnected components such as a battery, wires, electromagnet, etc. to create the entire telegraph system.

There were no email messages until I created the first email system in 1978, which I called "email," that was an interconnection of many components mimicking the paper-based interoffice memo system. We all know that a telegram is different from a tweet message, which is different from a text message. To send a tweet, one needs Twitter --- the system for sending tweets. To send text messages one needs the SMS system. And, to send email messages, one needs an *email system*.

Understanding what the inventors and pioneers actually invented relative to the third column of the above chart, in the rich lineage of modern digital messaging systems, is informative for understanding what email *is not*.

Early Digital Short Messaging System

In this context, the three key pioneers of digital *short messaging systems* that should be acknowledged as "inventors of text messaging," are Tom Van Vleck, Richard Kleinrock and Ray Tomlinson. Similarly, the two key pioneers of *digital community messaging* systems, David Wholley and Pat Doherty should be acknowledged as - "inventors of wall posts and blogs." Mistakenly, *Wikipedia* which erroneously and nebulously defines email as: **"... a method of exchanging digital messages from an author to one or more recipient"** has also attributed the invention of email on to these men, and this requires clarification. Such definitions are misleading.

Wikipedia lumps short messaging, community messaging, and intimate (formal) messaging together. This would be like *Wikipedia* defining a *letter* as: **"... a method of exchanging handwritten messages from one author to one or more recipients."** With such a definition, we would consider the sticky note, a bulletin board and a letter the same thing, since they all exchange handwritten messages from one author to one or more recipients. Clearly, they are very different and for different uses.

The innovations of these pioneers prior to my invention of email in 1978, though important, were not email. In fact, these pioneers had no interest in creating email. The leading researchers of that time had thought it "impossible" to create email --- an electronic system to mimic the paper-based interoffice letter/memo system. David Crocker, an Internet historian and a pioneer in electronic messaging, summarizing the state of electronic

29

messaging in December of 1977, in a RAND Corporation Report, Framework and Function of the MS Personal Message System, made this crystal clear:

> "At this time [December, 1977], no attempt is being made to emulate the full-scale, inter-organization mail system. To construct a fully-detailed and monolithic message processing environment requires a much larger effort than has been possible."

> "In addition, the fact that the system is intended for use in various organizational contexts and by users of differing expertise makes it almost **impossible to build** a system which responds to all users' needs. Consequently, important segments of a full message environment have received little or no attention."

During the 1960s and 1970s, text messaging pioneers Van Vleck, Kleinrock and Tomlinson were focused on sending simple text messages on a single computer and from one computer to another. They did much of their work when computers were centralized and connected to terminals and keyboards. A single centralized computer had multiple "dumb" terminals attached to it, like a hub and spoke. The hub was the central computer and the spokes were the individual terminals. Tom Van Vleck originated the first method for transmitting a text message between from *one user to another user* when both were connected to the same computer.

This early text messaging system was programmed on the CTSS (the "Compatible Time-Sharing System") mainframe built and operated at MIT from 1961 to 1973. Richard Kleinrock took the next step by developing a method to send strings of text commands across *two different but connected* computers. As the number of computers grew (with each computer having multiple users), Ray Tomlinson used the @ symbol (now used on Twitter, the modern text messaging platform) to distinguish a computer on a network, and to send simple text messages across multiple users connected to multiple computers, by appending text to a remote file.

Van Vleck's text messaging invention began with communication of text messages for *multiple* users on *one* computer. This led to Kleinrock's advances in communication of text messages across *two* computers, and then to Tomlinson's communication of text messages across *multiple* users and *multiple* computers.

Text messages were *not* email, just as sticky notes are not business or personal letters and memos. Email was the conversion of print letters and memos system to their electronic equivalents. Regarding his motivation for developing text messaging, Tom Van Vleck stated in 1964 that his focus was *not* on "letters": "The idea of sending 'letters' [or interoffice memos] using CTSS was resisted by management as a waste of resources."

Instead, Van Vleck focused on developing a system to transfer short text messages: "CTSS Operations did need a facility to inform users when a request to retrieve a file from tape had been completed." These "request[s]" were not letters or memos, but simple text messages.

In the winter of 1964, based on the growth of CTSS, which had hundreds of registered users and needed to provide support for remote terminals and discs, Louis Pouzin, Glenda Schroeder, and Pat Crisman proposed a new CTSS command called MAIL for communication of text messages between system users:

> "… a new command should be written to allow a user to send private messages to another user which may be delivered to another user at the receiver's convenience. This will be useful for the system to notify a user that some or all of his files have been backed up. It will also be useful for users to send authors any criticisms."

These "private messages" were modern equivalents of TXT or SMS, not letters or memos. The final implementation of MAIL by Van Vleck, on CTSS, required the input of these text messages as a sequential file, followed by project and programmer identifiers, both of which were numeric sequences. Van Vleck's MAIL command had all the essential features of a text messaging system: a source, an intended recipient, and a message. A later command was called SAVED, which worked with MAIL to provide one of the earliest forms of "instant text messaging."

The name "MAIL" for Van Vleck's early text messaging system was a concern to its authors. The name implied some relation to the USPS and to the business of print letter and parcel delivery. Van Vleck wanted to be clear that his MAIL was "messages." As he said:

"There was a lot of nervousness in the mid-1960s about ticking off the USPS. Calling our facility MAIL was thought by some to be a bad idea out of fear the USPS would require the destruction of a first class stamp for each message sent. If you put a personal note in a parcel, the rule then was that you were supposed to cancel and attach first class postage, because the USPS had a monopoly on mail transmission."

Despite the distinctions between the mainframe text messaging system of Van Vleck and the letter carrier work of the USPS, the name "MAIL" persisted. This was a source of the confusion in thinking that the lineage of Van Vleck, Kleinrock and Tomlinson created "electronic" mail or electronic "letters," when by their own admission they were not allowed to create "electronic" mail, and were focused on creating a system to transmit short text messages across multiple computers.

Versions of the "MAIL" nomenclature, however, were continued by other text messaging systems that were introduced to most of the early mainframes, CTSS's successor, Multics, re-implemented MAIL directly; BBN created "Mercury"; SDC's Q32 operating system provided DIAL. The time-sharing community was small in the 1960s, and idea sharing was common.

Text messaging platforms like MAIL evolved with the environments that housed them. Robert Frankston introduced the Send Message command to Multics

around 1970, removing the need to identify users on the mainframe by a numeric sequence. J. C. R. Licklider, in collaboration with Van Vleck, proposed introducing a version of MAIL to ARPANET, the precursor to the modern Internet, so that user text messaging could occur between physically distinct machines and not just among users of a single mainframe.

Early Digital Community Messaging System

Like the early text messaging systems for short messaging, digital community messaging systems such as networked bulletin boards developed in parallel trajectories throughout the 1960's and 1970's. PLATO, an early – and rather remarkable -- computer-based teaching mainframe developed by the University of Illinois in the 1960's, was home to the first digital bulletin board.

PLATO broke new ground, incorporating online message boards, multiplayer games, and chat systems into a mainframe architecture that allowed for simultaneous users, applet-like modules, and multimedia peripherals on relatively modest hardware. Even more impressive than its technical merits, however, was the strength of its community. For ten years, PLATO had more users than ARPANET, and software like David Wholley's 1973 PLATO *Notes* allowed users to communicate via a shared message board though potentially separated by hundreds of miles.

In the early 1970's, Pat Doherty wrote *Continuum*, later named Forum, an online bulletin board system for Multics that supported threaded discussions where one user could start a post and others could write back in a

"thread" of discussion. *Continuum* continued development as an internal Multics project, used as a platform to discuss system software changes and benchmarks.

Modern community messaging systems, including discussion forums in Lotus Notes, Facebook's Wall and comment-enabled Blogs, are the direct progeny of systems like *Forum* and PLATO *Notes*. An important property of all bulletin board and forum systems is a many-to-many connection scheme. While membership to such a community may be limited, discussion within such "walled" gardens is transparent. The power and flexibility of this many-to-many transmission scheme has played a significant role in human history: from the release of Martin Luther's Ninety Five Theses, and subsequent encyclopedic, papal response (spurred in large part by the development of the Gutenberg printing press) to the war fought with the Federalist and Anti-Federalist Papers in early colonial newspapers.

The strength of community messaging systems – from, blog posts to bug trackers – comes from uniform access. Intimate, one-on-one communication as afforded by email is discouraged by design, but trades this security and intimacy for transparency. These digital bulletin boards did not provide a radical new communication medium, but instead provided an augmented channel to support an already fundamental social activity.

These developments in short messaging and community messaging systems, though using the digital medium of computers and networks were different, and evolved along two different streams. In the late 1970s, the convergence of office automation and computing

resulted in the emergence of a third stream relative to intimate (or formal) messaging systems: email.

CHAPTER 2

The Invention of Email

I first heard the words "electronic" and "mail" linked together in 1978, when I was fourteen years old. For me, that linkage evoked the transporter on Star Trek dematerializing paper and beaming it across the ether. The concept of "electronic mail" was introduced to me by Leslie P. Michelson, PhD, a physicist from Brookhaven National Laboratory, who was at that time the director of the three-person Laboratory for Computer Science at the University of Medicine and Dentistry of New Jersey.

Michelson was a pioneer in bringing computers to medicine. My mother, Meenakshi Ayyadurai -- a mathematician, educator, and systems analyst in the computer department at UMDNJ -- had introduced me to Dr. Michelson hoping he would guide me academically and into a career. Earlier that summer, I had been admitted to a special program at New York University for introducing young people to the world of computers. NYU had received funding from the

National Science Foundation to develop an intensive introductory program.

New York University, in the heart of Greenwich Village, was known for artists, great ethnic food, creativity, and all sorts of spectacles. The only way to get there was to take a bus from my home in Livingston, New Jersey, to the Newark Port Authority. From Newark, I took the PATH train to New York Penn Station, and then the A train to Bleeker Street. If I missed the bus, which did happen at times, my poor mom would have to drive me at 5AM to the Newark train station.

There were forty of us who had been selected to the NYU program. The instructors were NYU professors and graduate students. The teaching was wonderful, and they exerted great effort to make the material understandable. In retrospect, having the opportunity to learn coding, programming, and digital circuitry in 1978 was an incredible good fortune. I remember painstakingly writing my first program in FORTRAN on punch cards. There was a true sense of wonder in seeing a set of instructions being carried out by a computer. The first programming assignment was to simulate a predator and prey relationship in an ecosystem.

Programming was also shown to have artistic applications. We were introduced to ARTSPK, an innovative language for creating drawings. A computer art competition was run to see who could create the best artwork. During this exercise, I had made a programming error that resulted in wild abstract shapes - - and my winning the award!

Upon completing the NYU program, I was taken on as a research assistant at UMDNJ in Dr. Michelson's lab. He was responsible for three mainframe computers, located on three separate campuses. UMDNJ was both a medical and a medical research facility, so thousands of medical students and doctors were spread across the campus locations in Piscataway, New Brunswick, and Newark. At each of the three locations, users accessed the local mainframe computers using keyboards and terminals, which were attached to a centralized mainframe machine.

At that time, the computers ran software to support various applications pertinent to running a medical school and supporting medical research. For example, there was software on the mainframe to do basic statistical data analysis for use by medical researchers. There was software for managing patient records and accounting information. In this model of time-sharing, each mainframe had various software applications. A user was able to access the mainframe through a terminal. They logged in to the mainframe, ran particular software, and logged out. Their user session on the mainframe was charged to their account at $.05 per minute.

Some scientists in Dr. Michelson's lab in Newark were writing new software for biomedical engineering applications. In this time-sharing networked environment of users spread across three campuses, Dr. Michelson asked me if I would want to build an *electronic mail* system—a system to create an electronic version of the interoffice postal mail system for managing the full range of creation, receipt, transmission, and processing

of paper memos within a user-friendly, network-wide, high-reliability framework.

Prior to that time, researchers had succeeded in building various components of systems necessary for creating such an email system. In the 1950s IBM had created FORTRAN, the first programming language. Others had created early database systems to store and retrieve information in the early 1960s. In the early 1970s, networking protocols were developed. However, no system provided anything like the full range of capabilities found in the interoffice mail system.

The interoffice mail system was the process, or *system*, for collaboration, communication and cooperation in the office environment. Within each office were a secretary (typically in the 1970s always a woman), and her command and control center was her *desktop*. The desktop was the actual top of a physical metal or wooden desk. On the desktop were various important objects: various bins (inbox, outbox, drafts), address book, paper clips, a typewriter, bond paper, carbon paper, etc. Behind the desk were typically heavy metal folders for storing files and memos. Below her desk was the trash bin.

The interoffice mail system had these physical analogs to many of the features and functions we see today in nearly every email program including the fields of the Memo containing the "To:," "From:," "Date:," "Subject:," "Cc:," "Bcc:," fields, and attachments to the memo of files and other documents.

In order to realize the scope of what email actually accomplished, it is important to look closely at exactly how the interoffice mail system worked.

Every office at UMDNJ had an address book, which listed each person's first and last names, campus location, group (e.g. surgery, pharmacology), room number and phone number. Address books were updated as employees came to and left UMDNJ. New people were added, and those who had left were removed. Periodically, a circular was sent out, which was the update to the existing Address Book.

Different locations had sorting facilities, where interoffice mail would arrive and be sorted by group, department, location, and office number.

Upon delivery, a secretary reviewed envelopes. An envelope intended for a single individual meant that the "To:" field would contain only one name. The secretary would also review the top portion of the envelope, including the "From:" and "Subject:" lines, in order to prioritize the envelope as one that should be looked at immediately, put aside for later review, or sometimes discarded altogether.

Sometimes a Manager would perhaps receive an important memo from a Director, and that Manager would want certain employees in his group to read it. The Manager would also want to know that they had in fact read it. Forwarding the memo with return receipt enabled the Manager to know exactly who got and who did not get the memo.

A memo sometimes would be edited after it was composed. Editing could be iterative based on the feedback received. Sometimes a memo would need to be sent to multiple recipients, not just one individual. This meant having multiple names of recipients in the "To:"

field. This was a complicated process, since copies had to be made – carbon copies on a typewriter.

A secretary would typically place dark blue carbon paper between two pieces of white paper and roll them into the typewriter, to create copies. The paper on top was the original, the one below was "Carbon Copy" or "Cc:" Sometimes, several carbons were used, and sometimes if the Cc list was long, the original would be mimeographed on a mimeograph machine. Then the first "To:" recipient would get the original, and each person on the "Cc:" list would get copies. This got more complicated if there were multiple recipients or a Group in the "To:" field.

The Sender kept a 'BCC' list in the header of the envelope only, and others who got Carbon copies did not see the one with the Bcc list. So only the sender knew who was on the Bcc list.

In the hospital environment, this was a very important feature, because certain envelopes had to be acknowledged as received. An envelope could be flagged as a 'Registered Envelope,' this would mean that it was treated differently for instance, the delivery person could put it in a different color envelope and ensured that recipient signed for it. When an interoffice mail system envelope was delivered, there was a formal receipt that would be signed by the recipient. This receipt would then have to be transported back to the original sender.

A 'check' mark was put next to each copy's intended recipient, so the envelope would be addressed correctly. Envelopes to be kept were often put into an archive file cabinet and organized for long–term storage.

Clearly, this was a complicated, labor-intensive process that served critically important purposes – but at a high cost in terms of time and effort.

So as a 14-year-old Research Fellow at UMDNJ, I was assigned by my supervisor Dr. Les Michelson to create an electronic version of the entire interoffice mail system. Right from the start I saw that it would be a daunting task. Furthermore, in the opinion of some people at UMDNJ it would be a waste of time. One of the doctors at UMDNJ told me, "What's wrong with paper memos? They're so easy to send. This email thing won't amount to anything. Email has no future."

I listened carefully to what he and others said. There would be resistance to the innovation I was trying to create for the secretaries, staff, and students at UMDNJ. Yet it was those very people who would most benefit from email. What would the new system have to do in order for them to start using it?

First, I had to offer them all the capabilities of paper-based interoffice mail, and much more: "Inbox," "Outbox," "Folders," "Memo," "Carbon Copies," "Address Book," "Attachments," "Groups," "Trash," "Compose," "Edit," "Sort," "Return Receipt," "Prioritize, " etc. -- altogether about a hundred different features and functions.

Second, I had better make email very user friendly. Technically speaking, all those features had to be delivered via a comfortable and compliant user interface. At that time there was no computer mouse, just a keyboard. An easy-to-use interface required simple menus, no need to type in commands or codes, simple navigation, and the ability to quickly scan incoming mail.

Third, the system had to be reliable. It had to work all the time. Just as the staff trusted their paper-mail system ("Neither sleet nor snow....") they would need to trust email.

The system I intended to create would have several other important elements as well:

A Rich Set of Features. The System would offer the ability to sort and view the Inbox and Outbox, to create Folders, even the ability to send Registered Mail! The System provided an editor, the ability to save a Draft, Send and Receive Messages. It also offered settings for Retries if there were Network Issues. Messages could also be archived, stored and deleted. I could not find any features that we have today, except for the mouse and graphical user interface that was missing in this first Email System.

Network Wide. The System enabled users to be resident across three geographical locations, each of which had three different servers (nodes) and multiple users at each location, with their own computers, connected to the servers. Various checks and balances were put into this first Email System for ensuring transaction of messages across locations e.g. if one server went down, what to do, when to resend, etc. Administrative tools and reports for managing network message transactions were part and parcel of email.

Security and Login. This system assigned each person a Username and Password. Most importantly, one could be at different locations and get their email. Each of the different locations had access to the Master User and Password tables, so users could seamlessly

move to different locations and access their email, something, which we take for, granted today.

Enterprise Email Management. Once such a system was built, many other administrative features were added, such as what to do if a person forgot their username and password, archival and retention policies, limits on how long an email message would be stored, when to clean up the system, etc. These were not always evident to the user, but on the back end of most systems such issues need to be addressed.

Database and Archival. Any system is not a System, without storage. This first Email System incorporated emerging database technology in a relational data store to index messages, users, and to sort and rapidly transact messages. The incorporation of such a sophisticated database structure provided the ability for this first Email System to offer many of the Rich Features described above.

Fulfilling these requirements became my passion. I wrote approximately fifty thousand lines of computer code, across a system of thirty-five interconnected software programs, and my work seemed to pay off. And, I named this system "email," a term I created. Though the term seems obvious today, in 1978 it was not. I selected the term since the FORTRAN programming language allowed only 6 characters all of which needed to be in upper case and the Hewlett-Packard operating system known as RTE-IV had a further limit that software programs could only be 5 characters: thus, "EMAIL."

The UMDNJ community began to adopt email, the electronic version of the interoffice mail system, and the term "email" came into use at UMDNJ and beyond. When I enrolled at MIT, the school's official newspaper – *The Tech* -- had a front-page article featuring the achievements of three incoming students. The invention of email was one of the three. In 1982, I received a copyright for "Email" from the US government. Copyright was the only protection available for software inventions at that time. Only in 1994 did the Federal Court of Appeals recognize software as a "digital machine" and allow it to be patented.

When I was working on my email project, I had goals in mind that were not merely technical. I wanted to create a system that would make life easier for all the office workers at UMDNJ. I can't say that I had a fully developed Marxist analysis of that workplace, but I was aware that the secretaries and other assistants were called upon to perform many mind-numbing tasks. The interoffice mail system required lots of copying, stuffing envelopes, typing additional memos, and so forth. I could not have put it into words at the time, but I did see this work as a revolutionary enterprise. I was proud I had that opportunity, and I'm still proud of that today.

Because some controversy has arisen surrounding my invention at UMDNJ – more on this below – I want to get a few things on the record now. If we recall, the RAND Report authored by David Crocker, in December of 1977, was clear that the pioneers in electronic messaging prior to 1978 had no interest in creating email. They had thought it "impossible."

I'm, however, gratified that my mentor at UMDNJ, Dr. Leslie P. Michelson, has also used the word "impossible" but with a very different intention:

> "Shiva did the impossible. He did precisely what early pioneers in electronic messaging, simply had no intention to do. Shiva invented email, which was the 'full-scale emulation' of the interoffice, inter-organization paper-based mail system, with the clear intention 'to construct a fully-detailed and monolithic environment' that could be used in 'various organizational contexts and by users of differing expertise'. Email is not the simple exchange of text messages. That dates all the way back to the telegraph and early developments in the transfer of electronic messages across computers using cryptic codes not usable by ordinary people in the 1960's and early 1970's. That is not email."

> "Let us be clear that mail is something far more complex than the exchange of text messages. It's about time we all realize these facts, and accept the reality of his incredible innovation. It's black and white. There is no 'gray' area here, except for the one created by those who will benefit from crediting email's invention to people and organizations that simply did not do it."

Finally, and again for the record, here is a statement by Noam Chomsky, professor of linguistics at MIT and one of the most renowned names in the entire history of his field.

> "The angry reaction to Shiva's invention of EMAIL and the steps taken to belittle the achievement are most unfortunate. They suggest an effort to dismiss the fact that innovation can take place by anyone, in any place, at any time. And they highlight the need to ensure that innovation must not be monopolized by those with power — power which, incidentally, is substantially a public gift."

> "The efforts to belittle the innovation of a 14-year-old child should lead to reflection on the larger story of how power is gained, maintained, and expanded, and the need to encourage, not undermine, the capacities for creative inquiry that are widely shared and could flourish, if recognized and given the support they deserve."

Unlike text messaging systems or community messaging systems, email is an electronic system for managing delivery and receipt of letters and memos. It is the electronic version of the interoffice memo and postal mail system. This is why it's important that Wikipedia be corrected for accuracy. Wikipedia lumps short messaging systems for text messaging such as MAIL

(created by Van Vleck), and even community messaging systems for online bulletin boards such as PLATO as "email." This would be akin to equating SMS (short messaging) and Facebook (community messaging) with email (intimate and formal messaging).

CHAPTER 3

Who Didn't Invent Email And Why It Matters

In early 2016, in the midst of writing this book, the media was buzzing about Ray Tomlinson's death. The Raytheon Corporation was Tomlinson's employer. Raytheon took the occasion to blast out press releases that the "Father of Email" had died. The truth is that Ray Tomlinson is neither the father of email nor did he invent email. It is important that this false history and Raytheon's marketing campaign to obfuscate the facts, be addressed. Because it matters --- on many levels.

This chapter was therefore added prior to going to publication to provide further clarification on what Ray Tomlinson actually did and didn't do.

Immediately following the barrage of Raytheon's PR campaign to bolster a false history of Ray Tomlinson, Dr. Arvind Gupta, a world-renowned technologist and information technology advisor to the Indian government, wrote in India's eminent publication *The*

Business Standard to clarify Tomlinson's role relative to mine:

> "The world has been talking about email this week, after the death of American programmer, Ray Tomlinson, on March 5. Tomlinson has been variously called email's godfather, father and inventor, for having created a message transfer system between two computers in the same room in the 1970s."

> "He did this as an employee of a defense contractor. Most memorably, he is credited with having chosen the "@" sign. But remember Marconi, famous for inventing radio? The world later realized that Jagadish Chandra Bose was the real inventor. Email has an Indian-origin creator too: Mumbai-born V.A. Shiva Ayyadurai. "

> "Once again, top academics, including the venerable Noam Chomsky at MIT, have come forward to validate this. MIT's Noam Chomsky has this to say: 'Email, upper case, lower case, any case, is the electronic version of the interoffice, inter-organizational mail system, the email we all experience today -- and email was invented in 1978 by a 14-year-old working in Newark, New Jersey. The facts are indisputable.'"

51

As I shared in the previous chapter, I invented email in 1978 as a way to support women whose jobs required writing interoffice memos, and fast and efficient communication, collaboration and coordination among three campuses at UMDNJ.

Email was created to emulate the interoffice, inter-organizational paper-based memo system consisting of the now-familiar features of every email system: inbox, outbox, folders, attachments, and the interoffice memo template, TO:, FROM:, DATE:, SUBJECT:, CC:, BCC:, Return Receipt, Address Book, Groups, Forward, Compose, Edit, Reply, Delete, Archive, Sort and Bulk Distribution. I designed it to be accessible to ordinary people with little or no computer experience, at a time when only highly-trained technical people could use a computer.

The first several hundred email users at UMDNJ collaborated between those three New Jersey campuses across an intranet-like environment. At the time of my inventing email, there were no laws to protect software inventions. In 1981, as a 17-year-old, I complied with the laws of the land, pursuant to the Computer Software Act of 1980 that allowed me to protect my invention using Copyright.

It was not until 1994 that the United States Court of Appeals for the Federal Circuit ruled that computer programs were patentable as the equivalent of a "digital machine." Before that Copyright was the primary mechanisms of protection, making computer programming code equivalent to sheet music or art. The practical result of which is that on August 30, 1982, I was officially recognized by the United States

government as the inventor of email. This is legally and factually verifiable.

In addition to creating email, the software and system, I also created the word "email," as early as 1978, to name that system, the timing of which is verified by two of the world's most eminent dictionaries based on the linguistic dates of origin of the term "email. For example, the Oxford English Dictionary places the first date of origin of the term "email" as 1979, a year after I created email in 1978. Furthermore, with my Copyright of the system the word "email," more pervasively entered the English language as documented in the Merriam Webster Dictionary, which places the term's date of origin as 1982. This was the year in which I received the official U.S. government Copyright for Email.

As Dr. Gupta continued in his article:

> "Why does academic credit matter? Because the journey matters, the motivation matters and history matters to generations of inventors, dreamers and entrepreneurs deserve to know the truth. Big change happens in small places when opportunity meets people who are driven to find answers. That's how email, as we know it, came to be."

> "The story of email exemplifies the journey of a team that included a precocious Indian-born teenager, eager to be useful in America -- grateful for the later opportunity to earn four degrees at

MIT, after inventing and copyrighting the email system -- and human desire to solve problems."

"For far too long we have all been led to be believe that communication's greatest innovations came out of defense research, inspired by the needs of war. Great innovations can be inspired to advance life, not just retrofitted from defense technologies."

For me, it matters because I am a man of science, and reputation and collegiality matters. There is a powerful economic motivation to discredit me and rewrite the history of this innovation.

When my papers were received by the Smithsonian's National Museum of American History, thirty years later, on February 16, 2012, and after which a *Washington Post* reporter, wrote an article entitled, "V.A. Shiva Ayyadurai: Inventor of Email Honored by the Smithsonian," my journey perturbed Raytheon's multibillion dollar marketing myth that contends inserting the "@" sign between the username and the host server is equivalent to inventing email.

Raytheon is a major American defense contractor that competes in a robust and expanding cybersecurity market. In 2014, Raytheon won $260 million in cybersecurity business and cites "reputation" among "principal competitive factors" considered by customers. They proudly showcase their employee, the late Ray Tomlinson, as "the inventor of email," to establish this

"reputation," to acquire new clients who need to protect their email. They are now caught between the factual record and their marketing campaigns.

Raytheon and Tomlinson's supporters from the Advanced Research Projects Agency Network (ARPANET) coterie used the occasion of my gaining rightful credit to the invention of email, albeit after over 30 years of being a "humble Indian," to discredit me. They unleashed hell on the *Washington Post* reporter and forced her editors to correct the story with a completely nebulous correction that I was "…not the inventor of electronic messaging." However, I never claimed to be the inventor of electronic messaging, whose history goes back to the Morse Code telegraph of the 1800s. However, I am the inventor of email.

Gawker Media, a company known for writing inflammatory and pornographic content on their various blogs to generate clicks for their websites as a means of increasing visitors to their salacious content, also used the occasion to viciously attack me. One of the writers for Gizmod (a Gawker Media web site), following the initial *Washington Post* article, referred to me an "asshole," "dick," "fraud," and "liar" for asserting my rightful credit to being the inventor of email. This writer using an erroneous analogy hypothesized that just because someone created something called the "AIRPLANE" it did not mean that they invented the airplane since the airplane may have existed before. This vacuous and inane argument subsequently, along with defamatory comments, proliferated on the Internet, created massive harm to my reputation as an inventor and scientist.

Gizmodo's article resulted in emboldening racist bloggers to refer to me as a "curry-stained Indian who should be beaten and hanged," "nigger Indian" and other expletives.

The fact is that not only did I create the term "email" to name my invention, but I also had invented email. The insipid argument made in Gizmodo, however, reached millions who began to doubt the facts of what took place in 1978 at UMDNJ.

Recently, after many years of working hard to find an attorney who would take on Gawker Media, I was fortunate to get support from Charles Harder, an eminent litigator, who had successfully sued and won against Gawker Media for placing pornographic content of Hulk Hogan (aka Terry Bollea) on one of their websites.

Mr. Harder, clarified with great accuracy what Ray Tomlinson actually did, when he commented on May 2016 in ArsTechnica, following the filing of my lawsuit:

> "What Ray Tomlinson actually did was modify a pre-existing program SNDMSG, which was a local user electronic 'Post-It-Note' system, using borrowed code from CPYNET, a file transfer protocol. His modification allowed a user on one computer to append text to a file on another computer. The user had to type in cryptic commands to even make this happen. It's 'caveman Reddit,' not at all what we know as email. Shiva Ayyadurai wrote nearly 50,000 lines of code to emulate the whole interoffice email

system, the email we all know and use today."

The record shows, furthermore, that the invention of email was of no interest to Tomlinson or the ARPANET in 1977. As we shared earlier, the seminal RAND Corporation report summarizing the state of electronic messaging by David Crocker clearly concluded in December of 1977 "no attempt is being made to emulate a full-scale, inter-organizational mail system... The fact that the system is intended for use in various organizational contexts and by users of differing expertise makes it almost impossible to build a system which responds to all users' needs."

Moreover, the ARPANET brochure of 1978, and even the one of 1986 (eight years later) makes no reference to the word "email," "e-mail" or "Electronic Mail" in the brochure or the index of their brochure.

The truth is that inventors generally, and the invention of email specifically, exemplify the meritocracy-based process that has made America exceptional in the history of innovation and technology. America's inability to protect that process, and those inventions, is a national vulnerability in the competitive global marketplace.

Had public policy been in step with software innovation in 1978 and patents been allowed to protect the creation of a young 14-year-old, immigrant inventor, Raytheon's PR machine would find it difficult to confuse and diminish the importance of the first copyright for email, which at that time was the only mechanism to protect software inventions.

So in spite of the black and white facts that I invented email, called it "email," and received official recognition from the U.S. government as the legal inventor of email, Raytheon appears to be able to convince major media houses by just screaming louder than I ever could. The truth is that my experience, here and now, is a clarion call for Congress to undertake meaningful reform to ensure fairness and justice to protect inventors.

The email system I built was not a variant of the text messaging programs. Many systems already existed to support text messaging. But email emulated the architecture and interface of paper-based interoffice mail. It was an electronic letter through a dedicated email platform. Email is an exquisite confirmation of Marshall McLuhan's adage that the content of any new medium is the preceding medium: the content of email was the interoffice mail system, not text messaging.

I want to close this chapter with a final very important distinction between the invention of email and the text messaging systems with which it has been confused. This same point will also show the basic connection between email and other forms of human communication dating back many centuries.

The point is this. The invention of email took place in a collaborative, and highly socialized environment for the benefit of everyone there. The invention was specifically intended to help the staff, which was responsible for everyday tasks that, though they were routine, were labor intensive for the people who had to perform them. The fact that I was literally a child when I was assigned to invent email might be the strongest

evidence of the organic nature of that environment. Perhaps a talented child was also called upon to do the first cave paintings, or to invent a *cuneiform* alphabet for scratching messages on shards of pottery in ancient Babylon.

Contrast this was the origin of text messaging that we've discussed in the previous chapter. Text messaging emerged in a highly centralized, semi-military, chain of command environment. It was not invented to lighten the workload of secretaries. It was intended for sending terse commands between soldiers on a battlefield. The corporations that employed the creators of text messaging were the largest defense contractors in America, and they were about as different from a hospital in New Jersey as it was possible to get.

When we compare the beginnings of email with start of text messaging, I believe the different intentions and social context are as significant as any technical issue. I also believe the Raytheon Corporation would agree with me, except Raytheon and I draw very different conclusions. I'm glad that email was invented in a collaborative environment where the foundational mission was healing and health research. I believe this is and always has been the optimal setting for innovation.

Raytheon and other defense contractors have a philosophical (and financial) interest in the idea that the military-industrial complex is a fertile field for innovation. For their own good, they want us to think arms research creates great technologies, even if it happens by accident. We should keep pouring money into the defense budget because every once in a while we will get GPS, or Velcro, or email.

The idea of an immigrant kid in Newark, New Jersey, creating email is a catastrophe to these people. But it's not just about me. It is about preserving that centrality of the military industrial complex. But when people realize that huge innovations like email can be created by fourteen year old kids, they can also realize they don't need to spend enormous sums backing the military industrial complex.

My unwillingness to be a "good Indian" and sit back in a lotus position is about my commitment to inspire this realization. The fact is innovation can happen anytime, anyplace by anybody. As this book goes to publication, I believe I've made one significant step towards in this effort. My lawsuit against Gawker Media has been victorious. Gawker Media was forced to pay be $750,000 to settle my defamation lawsuit against them and also forced to delete the three articles they published against me.

As my attorney Charles Harder commented in a news article following this settlement:

In 1978, a 14-year old Indian boy from Bombay, India and Newark, New Jersey, was tasked with replicating—in electronic form—a secretary's office desk for managing the entire system of paper communications (inbox, outbox, folders, address book, attachments, etc.); the electronic system did not exist; young Shiva Ayyadurai created that system; it worked and was a huge success; he named it "email"; he obtained the first U.S. copyright to that invention, and the world's modern system of electronic mail was born. Dr. Ayyadurai went on to receive four degrees from MIT including a Ph.D.

CHAPTER 4

Private to Public

So, as should be clear now, email was born in the office environment for business use in a health sciences institution to support an existing ecosystem of collaboration and cooperation to replicate the features of the interoffice mail system in digital form. Email is not a by-product of war and the military where a very different environment of top-down, command-and-control communication motivated early work in rudimentary short text messaging systems.

From 1982 to 1993, the use email grew, primarily in such business environments. The number of email users went from hundreds to tens of thousands. In early 1993, I recall running a seminar in Cambridge and asking a crowd of about a thousand attendees, how many had an email account. Two people raised their hand. And, those two were working at Lotus, where they had an email system running within a private local area network (LAN), independent of the Internet. **To be clear, one doesn't need the Internet to run email.** The email

system at UMDNJ ran on its own private LAN and wide area network (WAN).

After 1993, however, the number of email users began to grow from tens of thousands to millions, and then to billions of people around the world. And that number, I am absolutely certain, includes you.

The primary reason for this explosion was the introduction of the World Wide Web (WWW), a revolutionary technological development created by Tim Berners-Lee, a British computer scientist. It's interesting to note that although Berners-Lee had conventional academic training, he created the WWW on his own, without attachment to any corporate or government sponsorship. Like the invention of email, this was an example of innovation "coming from anywhere" - sometimes from predictable organizations and individuals, and sometimes not.

Berners-Lee graduated from Oxford University and subsequently became a software engineer at CERN, an internationally known particle physics accelerator near Geneva, Switzerland. Berners-Lee became aware that the many scientists who visited the facility had difficulty sharing information.

As he later wrote, "In those days, there was different information on different computers, but you had to log on to different computers to get at it. Also, sometimes you had to learn a different program on each computer. Often it was just easier to go and ask people when they were having coffee..."

Although millions of computers were already connected through the Internet, Berners-Lee saw that their ability to share information could be exponentially

improved through the emerging technology of hypertext. In March 1989, he described the concept of the World Wide Web in a proposal at CERN very simply titled "Information Management." Although the proposal was (incredibly) not accepted, Berners-Lee continued to work on his idea, and by late 1990 the three fundamental technologies of the World Wide Web were operational:

- HTML, an acronym for Hyper-Text Markup Language. This was the Web's basic formatting language.
- URI, or Uniform Resource Identifier, the individualized electronic address that identifies each resource on the Web.
- HTTP, or Hyper-Text Transfer Protocol., the technology for retrieving linked Web resources.

In 1991, the first Web pages appeared on the Internet. As with email, the initial motivation for the World Wide Web was to make online work easier and more efficient for as many people as possible - which turned out to include literally billions of people around the world. From the beginning, the World Wide Web was intended for use by anyone in any location and for an infinite number of purposes, without cost and without permission from any authority. The principles of the World Wide Web included the following:

- Decentralization: No permission is needed from a central authority to post anything on the Web. This also implies freedom from indiscriminate

censorship and surveillance. (But this is changing!)

- Non-discrimination: Access and connection on the Web should not be limited or enhanced by the fee paid to various service providers. The concept that everyone should be able to communicate at the same level is also known as Net Neutrality. (This is also changing!)

- Consensus: In order for universal standards to work, there had to be universal agreement to use them. Tim Berners-Lee wanted this by making the creation of standards a participatory enterprise. (But if ever this was possible, it almost certainly will not be done in the future.)

Tim Berners-Lee demanded that CERN agree to make the underlying code of the Web available on a royalty-free basis to everyone, forever. When this was announced in 1993, it began a period of creativity, collaboration, and innovation on a scale that had never before existed in all of human history.

When the World Wide Web was released, with its graphical user-interface, email's user demographic expanded from office workers to literally everyone. Email went from being run on private networks to quasi-public networks. I say "quasi" becomes these networks are publicly accessible but still owned by major telecommunication corporations, government and academia.

Web-based email programs such as Hotmail, Yahoo, and especially Google's Gmail enrolled hundreds of

millions of users. The WWW made email accessible to the masses and made it a consumer application. Anyone could get an email account. Even during this explosive growth of email, experts predicted the future of email as "dead." They predicted that instant messaging and online chat would kill of email. Or texting on smartphones would do it. Or, social media such as Facebook and Twitter would be the killer of email.

But when we look back at the model for email -- the interoffice mail system, which was a primary communication tool for businesses -- it becomes clear that, at the very least, email will be here as long as businesses are here. In other words, email will be here for a very long time.

However, not everyone, even in leadership positions in both government and technology, in spite of the ubiquity and explosive growth of email recognizes its permanence. For example, in 2012, Postmaster General Patrick Donahoe was a thirty-five-year veteran of the U.S. Postal Service (USPS) who managed the organization primarily using fiscal solutions, not through vision or innovation.

Donahoe did not really see the USPS as an opportunity for innovation and freedom to expand USPS' role to provide email as a real public USPS branded service versus a quasi-public service. Over the years, starting in 1993, when email began to cannibalize snail mail, in the new environment of the World Wide Web, Donahoe never chose to lead the USPS away from the physical into the digital. Instead, he continued to emphasize non-digital services like Priority Mail and First Class mail for cash flow.

USPS officials were happy to be generating revenue from their consistent portfolio of traditional non-digital products. But email was right there waiting for them if they had just wanted it, and if they had the imagination to fulfill the USPS brand promise. Email was a postal mail system in electronic form -- received, sorted, and transmitted with reliability, speed and efficiency- the core functions of any communication service. The problem was that the USPS saw itself not as a communications organization but as a paper mail delivery company.

At that time, I felt there was still time for the USPS to play a major role in email. Because of its trusted brand position, the USPS could offer public email and email management services to millions of businesses overnight, generating enough revenue to cover costs and make profit without layoffs.

Why did none of this happen? First, there was basic misunderstanding of what email really is, as now hopefully made clear to you, from the early chapters. This ignorance was the reason that even a technology leader such as Marc Zuckerberg, the founder of Facebook, could make a comment like, "Email is dead." It's also the reason why the head of the USPS and executives of other companies failed to use email appropriately.

Email, in the way these people spoke of it, was becoming synonymous with real-time chat, text messaging, SMS, Twitter, online forums, discussion threads, blogs, and wall posts. Because of the misuse of the term "email" to also refer to erroneously as "electronic messaging," there would be no distinguishing

between email as a platform and email messages as a medium, which flowed between email platforms.

The phenomenon of proclaiming email's death was not new. I recall that as early as 1997, industry experts who are paid to watch and predict trends had started to proclaim that email was dead, with the emergence of each new form of digital text-based communications.

For example, in the late 1990s, they were sure that real-time "chat" would replace email. Since then, there has been a consistent stream of news heralding the death knell of email at the inception of each new media. When Zuckerberg made his "email is dead" proclamation, he had a clever but unspoken motive. While he was declaring email was dead, he was fully integrating email into Facebook to foster what he called conversation. He saw that email was necessary for the "stickiness" he needed to keep his viewership from moving to Google+, through which Google was integrating social media features into Gmail, its pervasive email application.

Zuckerberg's comment was not really about email dying, but about attacking Gmail, which "owned" the email brand. He was really trying to say was that he hoped Google would die, once he incorporated email into Facebook. Zuckerberg, unlike the industry analysts who were truly misinformed about email, knew the power of email and the fact that social media needed it - which was why he was incorporating email into Facebook.

Furthermore, whether he intended it or not, Zuckerberg's declaration resonates with the future of language itself. It points us backward toward a time when the ability of human beings to communicate with

67

each other was in its first stages. A hundred years ago, even an average person wrote and received many handwritten letters every week.

These were physical objects that expressed the individuality of the author in many different ways. While it's true that online communication has facilitated instant and effortless communication, it's also a fact that tweets, emojis, or even emails are not exactly eloquent means of communication. Will anyone ever read anthologies of someone's tweets and emails the way, at least in the past, people read collections of letters by Dickens or Hemingway? What are the political consequences of a medium that, by its very nature, limits the intentions and abilities of ordinary people to express themselves? We're going to find out.

Zuckerberg's comments and events surrounding the USPS situation gave me a sense of urgency to complete this book, though I'd been thinking about it for much longer. That urgency was not out of some parochial or possessive interest to save email, as its inventor. My intention was to clarify what email really is on a much deeper level, and to recognize its unique power for branding and building connections. I want email to be rediscovered in a completely new way, and to demonstrate why organizations such as the USPS should be providing email as an important tool for the protection of our democracy.

Trust me. Email is here to stay for a long time. The only question is, will its immense and unique power be applied for everyone's advantage in a democratic setting, or will that power be used for something with less positive potential?

A more legitimate discussion of email concerns not whether it has a future, but what that future will be like. Specifically, will email be "free" - and I don't mean free of charge. I mean, will such basic freedoms as security and privacy be protected on email, or will they be compromised, constrained, restricted, and even turned against us?

PART 2

Observability - Privacy For The Few

Confidentiality of mail was one of the founding principles of
many democratic nations including the American government.
But that was before email.

CHAPTER 5

Your "Free" Email

Billions of email messages are transacted every day, and the numbers are growing -- but almost none of those messages are confidential. Private companies and their employees can easily access your email and you may never know it.

When you signed up a free email service, for example, you explicitly traded your rights to privacy for that free service. It's all in the fine print of your contract. At any time, your email service provider can shut you down or sell you out. And there goes your "freedom."

This is obviously a very important point, so let's look at it more closely. An article in the online edition of The Guardian (4-15-2014) states the following:

> "Google has clarified its email scanning practices in a terms of service update, informing users that incoming and outgoing emails are analyzed by automated software."

"The revisions explicitly state that Google's system scans the content of emails stored on Google's servers as well as those being sent and received by any Google email account…"

"'We want our policies to be simple and easy for users to understand. These changes will give people even greater clarity and are based on feedback we've received over the last few months,' said a Google spokeswoman."

Do you realize what this means? Every single email that passes through Google's vast system is "scanned and analyzed." Of course, this is depicted as if it's being done for your own good. Analyzing your emails is supposed to provide Google with marketing information that can be passed on to advertisers, so that you can start getting marketing materials that fit your interests.

If you send an email to an old school chum about meeting up at the 25th reunion in New Jersey, you might find ads for hotels in New Jersey showing up on news sites that you frequently visit, or on your social media pages. Google's terms of service has stated:

"Our automated systems analyze your content (including emails) to provide you personally relevant product features, such as customized search results, tailored advertising, and spam and malware detection. This analysis occurs as the

content is sent, received, and when it is stored."

On at least one occasion Google's Gmail users filed a suit against the company around the issue of scanning and analyzing email. In response, Google invoked several occasions in which law enforcement accessed people's email without a warrant, leading to the conclusion that users have "no reasonable expectation of privacy" regarding their online activities.

In a lame attempt to make people feel better about this, Google has declared "no humans read your email or Google account information in order to show you advertisements or related information. Only an automated algorithm does that."

Regarding this, the website digitaltrends.com has described the situation very clearly:

> "This case is not about law enforcement, the NSA, the FBI, or any other government agency spying on your emails. Instead, this case is about a private company collecting user data for whatever purpose it sees fit – *a practice that, unless you take extra precautions, is happening virtually every second you are on the Web."*

Perhaps the first sentence of that quote should have read, "This case is not yet about government agencies spying on your emails" – because there's very little, if anything, to stand in the way of that spying.

I certainly had nothing like this in mind when I invented email in 1978, and I'm sure it wasn't Tim

Berners-Lee's intention in 1993 when he introduced the World Wide Web. Nor was it my intention when I created the automated email response system called EchoMail.

More on that in the chapters that follow.

CHAPTER 6

What The Mail Used to Mean

In the United States, the 1776 Declaration of Independence makes an extraordinary assertion. To my knowledge, nothing like it exists in any other nation. After proclaiming that all people are born with "certain inalienable rights of life, liberty, and the pursuit of happiness" the Declaration continues:

> *"To secure these rights [life, liberty, and the pursuit of happiness] Governments are instituted among men... When any form of Government becomes destructive of these ends, it is the right of the people to alter or abolish it...."*

Consider what this means. If and when the government is understood to be standing in the way of the rights of the governed, the people are not only allowed but are actually encouraged to abolish it! That abolition is designated as another right, just like life, liberty, and the pursuit of happiness.

76

The Founding Fathers of the United States established various institutions so that the rights enumerated in the Declaration of Independence could be exercised. One of those institutions was the United States Postal Service (USPS.) The mail service was not created just for sending birthday cards. It was meant to ensure the freedom of citizens to communicate privately, without government inspection or tampering.

The history of the American postal service was greatly influenced by Benjamin Franklin (who was a signer of the Declaration of Independence.) While the American colonies were still under British rule, Franklin was Postmaster General. But the British government, partly as a result of disclosures involving mail that had political content, dismissed him. Later, in 1775, Franklin was again named Postmaster General, this time by the revolutionary Second Continental Congress.

Franklin was clearly sensitive to the connection between the mail and freedom of expression in general. The Postal Service made it possible for all citizens to exchange mail at an affordable cost. Further, there were laws against the mail being read or opened by anyone, including agents of the government unless they obtained an explicit court order. An internal policing mechanism was established -- the USPS Office of the Inspector General (OIG) -- which monitors postal facilities.

However, in modern times, over the years, the USPS has diminished. A significant portion of its work, has in effect, been privatized by FedEx, DHL and other premium delivery services. But the biggest change by far has been the USPS inability to adapt to a new

phenomenon: the explosive growth of email, whose volume exceeded first class postal mail in 1997.

Most people, it would seem, believe that emails are simply first class letters delivered by other means. But there are some big differences. When you sign up for an email account with one of the "free" email service providers, you are presented with a long legal document, which few people read. That document outlines a "privacy policy" of the email server. But it's really the "lack of privacy policy," and that's a big change from the old fashioned, hard copy postal mail service of the USPS.

You do not have privacy with your email. You do not own your email in the way that a physical letter was "your" letter. When you send email via a free service, it is not your exclusive property or the property of the recipient. It is available to anyone who has the means and inclination to read it, copy it, forward it, download it, edit it, or post it on Facebook for billions of other people to read.

When email surpassed postal mail volume, the USPS should have embraced the change and, in electronic form, provided the same infrastructure as postal mail services. In 1997, when I was Chairman & CEO of EchoMail, Inc., I had urged USPS senior management to offer email as a public utility. But the response was, "We are a $50-billion-dollar enterprise with more employees than WalMart. Why should we get into the email business?"

Let me offer an answer to that question. Email should be a public service administrated by the postal service because that's the best chance we have for

keeping some level of accountability and privacy for our online communications. Email should be subject to the same safeguards that apply to first class letters. That, in a nutshell, is why the postal service should get into the email business. In fact, in my meeting with the Postal Service back in 1997, I even offered them a business model, whereby they could potentially charge $50 per year for such a service. My view is that most Americans would pay for such a service given their email and any potential tampering by humans or otherwise would be protected by a public legal framework.

The irony of the Postal Service is that, nearly 15 years after I had urged them to get into the email business, in the Fall of 2011, the Postmaster General Patrick Donahoe announced that Postal Service was on the verge of bankruptcy. I was interviewed by *Fast Company* and *Time Magazine*, in which I shared my earlier 1997 discussions with the Postal Service. Had the Postal Service listened to me, I shared, they could have generated billions in revenue and would not be dealing with going bankrupt. My articles in those publications were critical and attacked the short-sightedness of the Postal Service executives.

My criticisms, however, did not fall on deaf ears, this time. In December of 2011, I received a call from the Inspector General of the OIG --- the organization that watches the activities of the Postal Service management. They were open to hearing my criticisms and ideas for how the Postal Service could generate new revenues. They formally funded two (2) research grants for my Email Laboratory, which I had founded within my research and educational institution, the International

Center for Integrative Systems. Our research executed a detailed analysis, and provided two reports detailing new ways on how the Postal Service could use email and digital communications to generate billions of dollars of new revenue.

Our reports were submitted in 2012 and 2013. The Postal Service moves slow. Public pressure obviously provides them an incentive to move faster. In front of them are multiple solutions to protect the public's email and ways in which the Postal Service can generate billions in new revenue.

Will they do anything about it?

CHAPTER 7

Innovation and Corruption

For me, helping the USPS was personal. My own struggle against the corrupt Indian government in 2009 to unleash freedom for Indian scientists to innovate had taught me the close link between innovation and freedom. In 2008, I had gone to India on a Fulbright Scholarship Program to study traditional systems of Indian medicine from the perspective of modern systems biology.

After completing my Fulbright Scholarship Program in India, I was recruited by the Office of the Prime Minister of India to head up a new initiative within the Council of Scientific and Industrial Research (CSIR), India's largest scientific institution, to drive innovation among its 4,500 scientists across nearly forty national laboratories. This new initiative would be known as CSIR-Tech. I would be its CEO and my role would be to identify and facilitate the spinning out of new scientific innovations -- innovations that had just been sitting in the lab -- to the general population of India.

The idea was to expedite the transition from the lab bench to the masses.

Jawaharlal Nehru, India's first prime minister, created CSIR to be a translational institute to innovate technologies and solutions to serve the broad masses of Indians. It was not supposed to be some academic institution writing and publishing papers or simply registering patents. But after nearly seventy years, it had devolved into an organization for publishing papers of questionable integrity, and for filing patents, less than 5 percent of which were of any value, to create an archaic system of promotion that enabled nepotism and obsequious behavior. This had no connection with the original mission of Jawaharlal Nehru, which was to innovate new technologies to serve the masses of Indians. During those nearly seven decades, moreover, CSIR had produced a paltry $2 million in revenue from its patents, less than $25,000 a year, while consuming tens of billions in public money, with significant portions of it routed through illicit means for self-serving purposes.

In my new role, I had also been officially appointed as an Additional Secretary within the Government of India as well as Scientist Level H, the highest grade of scientist within the Indian science bureaucracy. This role had within it many of the benefits including a bungalow in one of the elite areas of Delhi, a chauffeur, servants, and a reflective response of respect and honor by others for simply having the role. These I found frankly more of a hindrance in getting work done.

For me, I saw the role, however, as an opportunity to give back to my motherland --- the land that my poor

grandparents as farmers had toiled to earn a subsistence wage. Within three months, I developed a strategic plan for unleashing innovation from those labs by implementing an entrepreneurial program. I visited Indian scientists all over the country, and I met people who were absolutely brilliant. Amazing innovations were being developed. But administrators and bureaucrats who were jealous and afraid were sidetracking these innovations. There was a high level of corruption.

What I witnessed as I visited labs and met nearly 1,500 scientists was a consistent theme: the lab structure was set up as a continuation of the feudal system left by British colonialism. There were many incredibly smart scientists and innovators, who were trapped by this feudal and oppressive leadership structure.

If one studies Indian history carefully (as I had the opportunity to do while an undergraduate at MIT with Noam Chomsky), it becomes clear India never really got Independence. Instead, India transferred power from "white men who wore crowns" to "brown men who wore white hats," as denoted by the *Transfer of Power* documents signed between the new Indian ruling elite and their British brethren. Unlike America, there was no Declaration of Independence, clearly defining a new nation independent of the British crown.

The Indian bureaucrats continued to run India's internal machinery in the same resolute manner as the British feudal system of patronage, at best making India a flawed democracy, with little transparency and openness, the necessary ingredients for innovation. In some ways, the new "brown masters" were harsher to their Indian subjects than the British who left.

The labs within CSIR reflected this. And this is why relatively little innovation was taking place in those labs. Since the so-called Indian Independence of 1947, for nearly seven decades, not one Indian scientist had won a Nobel Prize *while living in India.* Ironically, the two Indian scientists who ever won Nobel Prizes while living in India, won them during pre-Independence, Colonial India, prior to 1947, during British occupation of India! Only after immigrating to America did Indian scientists seem to flourish in the relative freedom and merit-based opportunities offered by the American system of democracy. Har Gobind Khorana, an MIT professor, for example, was not even able to a get job as an instructor in an Indian educational institution. After coming to America, Khorana not only became a full professor at MIT, but also went on to win the Nobel Prize in Medicine. There are many such stories.

In October of 2009, after my deep frustration with CSIR and in solidarity with the 4,500 scientists of India, I published a nearly 50-page report called "The Path Forward." The first half of the report described what I had observed within CSIR: the rampant corruption, the feudal order which suppressed the creativity and innovative capabilities of brilliant scientists, a system which recognized obsequiousness over competence, and barriers that inhibited the ability for innovation to be translated to the public.

The second part of the report provided tangible and viable steps the CSIR administration could take to effect change and to unleash innovation across the CSIR labs.

I distributed this report in draft format via email to all the scientists across CSIR to gather their comments.

After all, I had wanted this to be a transparent, collaborative and cooperative effort in addressing the problem itself. However, within hours of publishing this report and transmitting it to the scientists, my email was shutdown. Then within a few days, I was fired, and ousted from my government house. Clearly, the CSIR administration did not believe in such transparency.

Death threats followed, and also threats from the Director General to reporters of major papers: they were not to share the facts. I was forced to flee India on a dramatic journey that included a 32-hour train ride to the Nepal border and four airplane flights before I was finally back home in Boston. Major newspapers, including the New York Times, covered the events of my dismissal, in spite of threats from the Director General of CSIR on NY Times reporters not to share the facts.

So much for freedom in India! So much for innovation! Subsequently, I wrote an invited Commentary article for India's *Nature* magazine, entitled "Innovation Demands Freedom: Why America Innovates and India May Never," in which I laid out my thesis that without Freedom there cannot be Innovation in India, along with the details of the corrupt behavior I observed. The Indian government banned this article and demanded that Nature remove it, under threat of a libel suit. *Nature*, fearful of libel laws in the United Kingdom, complied. However, by then, the article was across the Internet for everyone to read.

So for me the USPS was an amazing institution—representing the fusion of *Innovation* and *Freedom*. From my experience in India, the failure of an institution such

as the USPS would be significant—it would send a global and reactionary signal, and a blow to those core elements of innovation and freedom, inherent to the foundations of America's inspiring developments in science, technology, and the arts. The USPS had to re-innovate itself, for it was not just a mail communications company but also a symbol of that freedom and democracy. The USPS was borne out of the American revolutionary war against British colonialism, and it afforded each citizen the incredible innovation of the postal mail system, where every citizen could communicate across space and time, to send mail anywhere, connect with loved ones, business associates, and friends, for pennies, no matter what their background.

Such an institution was about providing the fundamental tool of democracy: the right to communicate freely.

Our public institutions, which emerged out of hard fought freedoms, need to keep up with technological innovation be it in India or America. Otherwise, their inertia and corruption, explicit or implicit, threaten our freedom. The subversion of email by private companies is an example of what happens when such inertia sets in. Our "free" email systems, now controlled by private companies, when the Postal Service (the public) should have owned it, are a deplorable failure of the public trust.

The once trusted brand of the USPS made people feel comfortable, knowing any mail sent or received was handled with care and security. Our local postal worker was a symbol of that trust that implicitly connected each citizen directly to the fabric of the hard-fought gains of

the American Revolution. That trust now needs to be re-established for liberty to prevail.

It is we as citizens and as individuals who must fight to re-establish the protection of our communications. This struggle for freedom and protection of our communications will not be easy because of the vested interests who have much to gain. I do know from my own personal struggles that truth and freedom are possible when we do not give up. In my case, relative to India, in 2015 news anchor Arnab Goswami on Times Now channel, which reaches tens of millions across India, finally exposed what I had endured in being hounded out of India for exposing the truth about the corrupt CSIR. This was a major vindication.

We have no choice, but to fight if we want to secure our freedom.

CHAPTER 8

Hillary's Email And
The New Caste System

In 1970, when I was seven years old, my family left India to the United States. We were a "low caste" family and departing India was an attempt to leave the Indian caste system behind.

But, what about the American caste system? Is there such a thing? While some of the cruder elements of caste do exist in the United States, this country is certainly much more flexible than India has been. But new markers of caste are emerging in America, often without people recognizing them for what they are.

Consider privacy, for example. As technology advances and other social changes take place, privacy is becoming an exclusive prerogative of the rich just as membership in exclusive clubs has been in the past. Absence of privacy, on the other hand, is becoming the general condition of most people's lives.

Make no mistake: whatever the average American is doing — whether it's online or driving down the street –

it is fully observable by government or corporate monitoring. Virtually every square inch of public space in our large cities, interior of exterior, is videotaped. Every piece of first class mail is photographed, and every email is visible to the service provider – forever — and also visible to anyone else who has an interest in reading it, whether legally or otherwise.

It's sometimes been mentioned that the defining characteristic of prison is the total absence of privacy. But in that respect, the difference between prison and everyday life is becoming only a matter of degree. Gated communities, private planes, private schools, private clubs, private banking – these are available to our American Brahmins, and most definitely not available to our millions of lesser breeds.

Freedom of secure and private correspondence was won in the American Revolution. But today, in the "free" services of digital communication, that freedom simply does not exist. And it's not getting any safer for first class mail either.

Some historical perspective can help to clarify this. During the Prohibition Era of the 1920s and early 1930s, the government was finding it difficult to prosecute highly sophisticated bootleggers. They not only understood how to physically evade the police in the creation and shipment of liquor, but they also knew how to successfully defend themselves in court if they did happen to get caught.

In response, the government began to use some new strategies. Instead of directly accusing the bootleggers with alcohol-related crimes, charges like tax evasion, "crossing state lines," and "using the mails for fraudulent

purposes" proved successful. You could go to jail if it could be shown you sent the wrong thing in a package or letter, and you still can.

The US mail, which had been intended as a highly confidential medium even for revolutionary documents, has become another opportunity for government control. This has vastly expanded since the 9/11 attacks. It may be hard to believe, but today every single letter or package sent through the US mail is photographed. Opening the letters without a court order is still prohibited, but just knowing who's writing to who is a powerful surveillance tool.

What would Ben Franklin have thought of that? I know my own feelings about the USPS as a possible safe haven for email have changed, and I haven't exactly become more optimistic, but have realized that we as citizens need to exercise our rights to ensure that our government institutions such as the USPS live up to their promise and serve us. The good news is that we can do this as taxpayers for such publicly-funded institutions, however, it's much harder to exercise our rights with a private company.

In 1997, I had recommended to the USPS that email should be provided as a public utility, just as the federal government provides mail service or interstate highway and water systems. I also pointed out that, if there were a small fee for using email, this could be a valuable source of revenue for the government because of the vast number of email users.

Even as late as 2011, I was interviewed by *Fast Company* magazine about these possibilities:

"Is it too late for the USPS to capitalize on email now? Regardless of whether the USPS stays public or is completely privatized, Shiva Ayyadurai believes it can save itself by creating and selling, not just using, digital communications technology. He says, 'The U.S. Postal Service could offer an email management service to millions of businesses overnight, generating enough revenue to cover costs and make profit without layoffs. Global 2,000 companies and small to medium enterprises alike sorely need email management, which is a massive opportunity. They could also lead the charge in email validation and other solutions for a host of problems faced by email marketers.'"

Along with solving its fiscal problems, I thought the USPS could instill and enforce the privacy of email just as it does (or so I assumed) for first class letters. But today we can no longer simply accept that the government will follow its promise to the public and insure privacy any more than we can look to private companies such as Google or Apple to do so.

If the government were to express interest in email today, I could not resist the suspicion that there was some undisclosed policing agenda behind that interest. How can anyone have faith in the government regarding the right of privacy after Julian Assange and wiki-leaks, and the revelations of Edward Snowden about the

National Security Agency? Despite what I thought in 1997, expecting the government to protect email communication has become a case of the fox guarding the henhouse.

This is the state of affairs Hillary Clinton seems to have understood very well. At the time of this writing, she has been under investigation for receiving and sending secret government documents using a private and exclusive email server. Ms. Clinton asserts this a misunderstanding on her part and that she was never trying to evade the lack of privacy that's built into email. She has said it was a mistake. She has said she is sorry and she won't do it again.

She might also have said that she believes in the Easter bunny, or something equally outrageous – and, to no one's surprise, she is not going to be prosecuted for her obvious wrongdoings.

The reality is, Ms. Clinton understood the vulnerability of email messages and looked for a way around that. I shared this in an August 8, 2015 interview with *The New York Times*, an excerpt of which is shared below:

> "So there may have been other reasons for using a private server. For an oft-attacked politician considering a presidential run, the server would give Ms. Clinton some control over what would become public from her four years as the nation's top diplomat. 'I've been following it very carefully,' said Shiva Ayyadurai, an email pioneer who has designed email systems for both government and large

corporations. A private system, he noted, 'would make it possible to decide what would be disclosed and what would not.'"

But not everyone has that level of understanding, much less the resources to set up a private email server to protect their email. If this story were to have a title, I would suggest The Triumph of the Oligarchs. It's a story with a happy ending for the privileged class of people who are deemed "too big to fail." They're not subject to constraints on privacy like Google's "terms of service" that are imposed on everybody else, even though everybody else isn't even aware of it.

The elites, like Ms. Clinton, can find ways to short-circuit laws and create a gated community of privacy for themselves while the rest of us will have to deal with un-private "free" email services.

I wish I had a simple solution for these issues. I would love to paint a "happily ever after" landscape for the future of email, but I won't attempt to do that in these pages. Doing so would be dishonest, and the picture itself would undoubtedly have many inaccuracies.

Instead, I can depict possibilities for the future of email, even if they aren't "happily ever after." Maybe they will be. Maybe they won't. But we are definitely in the midst of the greatest revolution in the history of human communication since the invention of the printing press. And it's just getting started.

So it's hardly a surprise that Hillary Clinton would feel entitled to a private email server, and let others be damned. It comes with the territory.

Give some thought to the presence (or absence) of privacy in your daily affairs, and see how that correlates with other areas of your life. You'll notice how privacy is indeed becoming a prized private pleasure of our upper castes. And if that angers you, think twice before writing any emails about it.

PART 3

Predictability - Control of the Many

Corporate America was slow to recognize email
as a business intelligence tool to predict and manipulate
customer behavior. But once that potential was realized,
email turned customers' messages into profits. Not that
there's anything wrong with that! But, did the customer
know what was happening to them?

CHAPTER 9

The Clinton White House

It feels like I can't get away from the Clintons and email. Even before my being asked to comment on Hillary Clinton's email scandal recently, as far back as 1993, I was involved with the Clinton White House. However, before I get into those details, let me provide a background on this part of the book. In addition to inventing email, working with the USPS to educate them on how to use email to serve the public and make money, I was the inventor of the first AI technology for analyzing and managing the growing volume of inbound email that the ease-of-use of email itself created. However, at the time of its creation, I had no idea of what I had actually invented. On some level, I have regrets.

What I had created with EchoMail was a way for major corporations, government and other businesses to understand your thoughts, what you were saying in your email, and then intelligently figure out ways, in an automated way to respond back. I did this initially to

save the effort of call center workers who had to mindlessly read inbound emails and respond to them manually one by one. However, what I had really created was a way for these large organizations to know you, and manipulate your behavior.

In this chapter and others in this part, I will provide a wide spectrum of case studies, so you can appreciate how powerful the AI technology such as EchoMail can be. My hope is that by sharing these case studies, as an "insider" who worked closely with these companies, you will wake up and become conscious of how you are not only being observed, but more importantly being controlled, one email at a time.

As we've seen in earlier chapters, in 1993, the Internet exploded with a communications revolution such as the world had never seen before. Until then, the use of email had been mostly confined to business or governmental use. But with the introduction of the World Wide Web, everybody could send emails to anybody they wanted. And, that's exactly what everybody did.

Before 1993, email was a business application. But then, suddenly, everybody was sending email messages. Politically, it was not a good idea to ignore any of those attempted communications. No matter how inconsequential they might seem, writing to the President was an important experience for a farmer sitting at a kitchen table or a student in a college library. So the Clinton White House had twenty interns who were sorting 5000 emails a day into 147 patterned categories including education, drugs, and many more.

In an attempt to bring this situation under control, the government announced a competition for analyzing and sorting the emails. No such thing had ever been done before, because there had been no need for anything like this. I entered the competition and was selected to provide the service. I won the contest, and it wasn't exactly a surprise. MIT had even re-named me "Dr. Email."

Before long, as I looked at thousands of emails a day, I had an important realization: they were not all that different. In fact, looking below the surface of the contents, the emails were almost robotically repetitious. I had done extensive academic work on pattern recognition, including the classification of people's handwriting. Now I was starting to recognize patterns of content in those thousands of emails. I suspected that content could be organized around a certain number of thoughts and ideas just as I had organized the physical properties of handwriting.

I created some algorithms to detect an email's essential features. I named the software Xiva, and founded a company called Millennium Cybernetics to market the idea. That was in 1994, a time when email was still in its infancy and major retailers were just starting to make full scale commitments to the Internet. Jeff Bezos wouldn't have launched Amazon.com until July of the following year.

When I learned that AT&T needed help with its surprising volume of email, I sought an introduction. No matter how Web commerce unfolded, I saw that big firms would get lots of online messages and would have to deal with them. After a pilot demonstration of Xiva –

which I trademarked as EchoMail -- AT&T signed on in 1996.

The basic principle for classifying and decoding email is surprisingly simple: human communication is not as diverse as we think it is. EchoMail scans emails for key words and phrases that characterize the few fundamental properties that are of interest to a company in any email.

For example, is the email about a billing problem, or a merchandise return, or a legal problem? EchoMail evaluates an email and sorts it in the correct category. The program does this by applying a dictionary of key words and word relationships known as a semantic network. If the program finds the word "website' and 'problem' close to one another, it might conclude that the email's issue is an online ordering problem. Depending on how an email is classified, EchoMail can choose either to reply from a selection of prewritten responses, or forward the message to one or more departments for humans to address.

EchoMail can also classify the email as negative, neutral, or positive by homing in on key words such as "terrible" or "superb." One message included the words "da bomb." EchoMail initially classified this as negative, but when we learned 'da bomb' means 'you're cool' we changed the classification. Finally, EchoMail can benefit marketing by classifying customer types. Email writers often give away such information as whether they own a boat, or their home address and zip code. EchoMail can add this information to the client's customer databases.

Eventually nearly every major Fortune 500 company adopted EchoMail to more effectively manage incoming electronic correspondence. EchoMail was in the right

place at the right time, and that time is by no means over. Today EchoMail is being offered to all businesses, small and large, and the need is greater than ever.

In the early 1990s, as this new era was dawning, the concept of pattern recognition was a hot topic. Pattern recognition was based on the principle that a foundational image would emerge from a large volume of data if all the distracting details could somehow be stripped away. Chaos theory, for example, proposed that seemingly randomized visual images could be simplified by changing the observer's point of view – as happens when you zoom out from an online map. The coastline of Norway might look jagged and without a pattern if you were sailing alongside it in a boat, but seen from a plane at thirty thousand feet a general outline will emerge.

The process of pattern recognition has three phases. We can speak of them in terms of face recognition, but the phases are the same in all applications. The first phase is *feature extraction*. What are the components of the material we're dealing with? With the coast of Norway, the features would be the hundreds of small inlets and harbors -- *fjords* – that give the coast its character. With human faces, the features obviously include the eyes, nose, mouth, and hair.

The second phase is called *clustering*. It's defining the relationship between the features in an objective way, so that groups of individuals can become recognizable based on those relationships. For instance, there might be a cluster of people whose eyes are between two and three inches apart, and those people might also tend to have wider mouths than other people. There might also

be many more people in one cluster than in another. Clustering is the phase that most people would clearly associate with pattern recognition.

Learning is the third and final phase. This means drawing meaningful conclusions from the earlier results. If you were looking for patterns among different kinds of snakes, for example, the feature extraction process would involve identifying the markers that define a snake – they all have two eyes, they all have some color or pattern on their skin, and they all crawl on the ground. The clustering process would then separate the snakes into different groups based on shared characteristics. Finally, the learning process would describe certain events or outcomes that correlate to different clusters – as, for instance, no one died who got bitten by a green snake with a round head.

One difficulty in the early science of pattern recognition – and artificial intelligence in general -- was a tendency to veer toward reductionism. It's great to simplify chaos, but it can also be oversimplified. Pulling back from an image can reveal its underlying character, but pulling back too far can make everything look the same.

CHAPTER 10

Reductionism and Beyond

In 1998, I was interviewed for an article in the *New York Times*. I provided some statistics and information about what was then called "electronic commerce." That meant phone calls and emails from customers to companies. According to the article, one unnamed consumer products company received 264,000 telephone calls to its customer service center in one month -- more than a quarter of a million calls! About 225,000 of those calls were processed in what the company considered a satisfactory manner.

During that same period in 1998, the company received roughly 20,000 email messages from customers. But while the "success rate" for processing phone calls was 85 percent, only 10 percent of the emails got replies, and sometimes there was no reply for several weeks.

The article further stated that the vast majority of companies operating websites at that time promoted themselves as offering customer service via email. But spot checks found that 30 percent of emails sent to

those companies never got any response at all. And when messages were sent to the customer service email addresses of two dozen leading consumer-oriented corporations, only seven of the companies responded in less than 24 hours, and five simply did not reply.

My quotes from the article highlight how far electronic messaging has come in the last twenty years. It's hard to believe major corporations did not take email seriously, but that was definitely the case:

> "'Before someone puts in our system,' said V. A. Shiva, president and chief executive of General Interactive, 'we ask them, Do you value Email? Do you have policies and processes for handling this inflow? Whose responsibility is this mail, marketing or customer service or someone else? What happens to a message, for instance, if it hasn't been read in five days?'"

> "Mr. Shiva added that the slow adoption of systems to handle incoming E-mail had 'a lot to do with technology but also with process and elevation of consciousness -- even politics going on within companies.'"

My challenge in those years was to adapt the emerging technology of artificial intelligence to the complexities of thousands of automated email responses in a real world setting. In the 1990s, the tendency toward reductionism turned the development of artificial intelligence into a search for "magic bullet" solutions

regarding everything from medical research to automated email responses. "Natural language technique and "neural network" technique were two potential magic bullets that proved less than magical.

By using natural language technique, a reader might confidently feel that the author of an email message is angry. But another reader might disagree, and argue that neural network technique must be used. But both readers would feel that there is a magic bullet solution that must be used.

I believed that the need to read and reply to emails could be addressed without pledging allegiance to any specific academic ideology. EchoMail's work for the Nike Corporation was an example of how this worked.

Nike had a large billboard ad with a picture of one of their shoes and an email address below it. There was nothing else on the billboard. The ad was plainly and simply an invitation for the public to send emails to Nike for any reason they chose. There was also a television ad with a similar layout and purpose.

Using advertising to incite people to write in email was unprecedented. Integrating with print and web was radical. No one had ever combined media in this fashion before. Did it work? Yes. Consumers wrote in by the thousands. When they wrote in, using the same EchoMail technology originally set up for crisis management, email was analyzed, routed and responded. The technology this time discerned the consumer's shoe of interest, and also extracted other valuable data.

How was this possible with hundreds of thousands of incoming emails? How could a company like Nike process all this? An email message has both strengths

and weakness compared to a typed letter, or especially to a handwritten letter. Since emails can be created very quickly, they can present ideas spontaneously and frankly, just as in a face to face conversation. Increasingly, people don't worry about grammar or punctuation. They just want to get their message across as quickly as possible.

EchoMail formed responses that were tailored to the incoming request and also provided a link in the response to a local shoe retailer who would likely have that product in stock. The idea was therefore to use TV and print to engage consumers to interact through email, and then to use the email response to drive consumers to the local store. Nike served as the intermediary between their consumers and customers. Consumers could communicate one-on-one through email and then engage with their local retailer. This campaign worked to close the loop between the end consumer, the product, and the retailer (customer) through an intimate interaction. In summary, broadcast media was integrated to drive one-to-one intimate email communications.

But email is also a very "flat" medium. Nuances tend not to come across very well. An email is not a good place for storytelling or sharing deep emotions. It's best for conveying facts and information in a straightforward, condensed manner. But that doesn't keep people from going off in whatever direction appeals to them. In writing to Nike, someone might start with message about how their sneakers don't fit, and then switch to a long narrative about a girls' soccer club or Nike's manufacturing policies. Anything was possible when

customers responded to the billboard ad, and EchoMail had to analyze those responses.

CHAPTER 11

Nike Wants You To Love Them

My work with Nike was one of the most gratifying and informative experiences of my career. If I had to name anything that has had a more transforming effect on society than email, I would have to say it's the running shoe. Without the running shoe, of which Nike was the most successful pioneer, America's whole orientation toward fitness and health which began in the 1970s could never have taken place. There would not have been millions of joggers, there would not have been thousands of people running marathons or joining fitness clubs, and there would not have been the sudden and intense interest in healthy eating. All that was made possible by the running shoe.

Nike is not only a company that experienced fantastic success, but also made its way through negative publicity that could have ruined a less resourceful organization.

The year 1997 could be remembered as "The Year of the Sweatshop." The world's biggest clothing manufacturers reeled as one public relations disaster after another took place. Article after article came out

exposing the horrendous working conditions, coupled with breathtakingly low wages, in the factories of some of America's most prominent brands. Even worse, the workers were often children, as young as thirteen, forced to work twelve-hour shifts, for up to seventy-five hours a week.

Workers making the talk show host Kathie Lee Gifford's clothing line earned $.31 an hour. The cohost of *The Morning Show* became an icon for the ruthless lipstick-clad capitalism practiced by American companies all over the world. Similarly, in the first quarter of 1996 Disney posted profits of $496 million and paid CEO Michael Eisner what amounted to $97,000 an hour. Meantime, all over the world, workers producing Mickey Mouse shirts were paid as little as $.16 per hour.

In this milieu, Nike was yet another American icon that came under fire that same year. Started by Bill Bowerman and Phil Knight in 1964, the company was founded on outsourcing: the idea that they could compete with the German brands which dominated the market by producing quality running shoes in Japan. With only $500 and a handshake deal, Bowerman and Knight ordered 300 pairs of sneakers, which Knight offered out of the trunk of his green Plymouth Valiant. When the shoes sold, more were ordered from Japan.

Eventually it became cheaper for Nike to build its own factories. By the 1970s it was too expensive to continue producing shoes in Japan, so Nike built plants in Korea, Malaysia, and Indonesia. Wherever Nike went, the economy boomed. This succession of investment, growth, and subsequent sale and resettlement was so solid that when financial analysts asked themselves

which developing economy was next in line to boom, they looked at where the sportswear company was building its newest factories.

1996 had been a great year for Nike. Stock price doubled. But then came the articles about sweatshops and how companies like Nike profited from them. When they were accused of using sweatshops, Nike's initial response was all but confused:

> "'It's an age-old practice,' said spokeswoman Donna Gibbs, '... and the process of change is going to take time. Too often, well-intentioned human rights groups can cause dramatic negative effects if they scare companies into stopping production and the kids are thrown out on the street.'"

Profits were going up, sales were going up, and Nike had just partnered with Michael Jordan on a new brand of sneakers. But in 1997, Nike learned a very expensive lesson on the power of new media and how bad PR spreads faster on the Internet. With earnings increasing to the tune of 40 percent, it was to be a record-breaking fiscal year. But the media storm did not let up. Anti-Nike websites sprung up all over the world. Using the Internet, activist groups could communicate and coordinate internationally, then organize locally to create worldwide "Anti-Nike Day" protests. This was long before Twitter and Facebook. The boycotts were effective, and sales soon started to drop. Stock prices plummeted. This spurred Nike to launch its own website, Nike.com.

Prior to 1997, communications for Nike had been in postal mail letters, which would get handled by their consumer correspondence team who would open each one and respond. They would also get phone calls, which were also treated by their consumer affairs staff. When they launched Nike.com, it marked the first time the company began receiving email. Nike realized that they would now have to offer real-time responses to this rapidly growing volume of inbound email. Emails were coming not only from their *customers* but also increasingly from *consumers* too.

Consumers were the end users, who actually bought and put on the shoes. Customers were the retailers to whom Nike sold their shoes for selling to the consumers. Previously, Nike mainly dealt with customers: these were typically stores such as Foot Locker that would buy in bulk to sell to the consumers. Now, because of email, consumers that previously dealt primarily with the retail stores were in a position to take issues up directly with the manufacturer.

This was radical and new, especially the volume of such consumer communication to Nike. This created a new issue for Nike, and Jane Flood was the executive who Nike charged with solving the problem. She would find her solution at a new media conference.

Tom Zawacki, one of the founders of Modem Media, the world's leading interactive agency at the time, was speaking at an Internet Sports conference when someone asked about technologies for handling email. Tom told the conference about EchoMail. This led to a series of phone calls with Nike representatives. Within

days of their seeing an EchoMail demonstration a contract to process Nike's email was drawn up.

There was a significant concern at that time about Nike's use of potentially unfair business practices. As thousands of email came in every day on the subject of sweatshops, each and every one of them could be answered quickly, cheaply, and effectively. Not only that, but with EchoMail, Nike was able to generate reports about who was sending those emails. EchoMail's technology analyzed the email across five content dimensions: attitude, issue, request, products, and customer category. For example, suppose someone wrote the following email:

> "I love your website and my new Air Jordan's, but I'm very upset with your labor practices. I am a CEO of a small company and would also like a copy of your annual report."

EchoMail would automatically analyze the content and characterize the attitude as *positive* and *negative*. In this case, the consumer is happy about the website and the Air Jordan's, but is upset about Nike's labor practices. The issue in this case would be *website* and *labor practices*. The request would be for an *annual report*. The customer type would be *CEO*. Finally, the product would be *Air Jordan*. EchoMail would save this data for each email, and then use this analysis for automatic routing to the right department, and would also propose an intelligent response, by piecing together existing response paragraphs (based on the content categorization), which it would then send to a customer

service representative for review, editing, and final transmission back to the consumer. All of this was tracked; so detailed reports could be created to know the pulse of the consumer in real time.

Phil Knight himself and his senior staff would regularly log in to EchoMail to get reports from the system. EchoMail also allowed Nike to organize those emails into groups, helping Nike address the individual consumers about their concerns by sending messages from corporate communications. These messages could relay the reality from Nike's standpoint on worker treatment as well as new programs Nike was implementing to ensure more favorable treatment of workers. Email was used to tell Nike's version of the story direct to the consumers—something they were not able to do before—one-on-one.

This power to directly respond to consumers was incredibly effective. Many other companies were simply ignoring email. Even in 2012, less than 30 percent of companies responded to their customers and consumers within forty-eight hours. Research reports show that there is an 85 percent chance of losing business if emails are not responded to within that forty-eight-hour window.

Nike used email to turn protesters into consumers. This not only proved the value of the EchoMail technology, but also the value of email as a direct one-to-one communications vehicle. Nike used the mined data from email communications to support Nike's brand by being proactive and being responsive to their consumer needs. Nike used EchoMail as an early warning system. Nike had always seen itself as creating products that

represented a marriage between technology and design. Nike realized that within the content of email there was opportunity to not only address a crisis but also the opportunity to really listen to consumers and formulate new products and designs faster and cheaper, from direct consumer feedback.

There are many uses for the data one can get out of email other than early warning systems and crisis communications. Email can be used as a sales tool. At the time, Nike spent half a billion dollars on traditional advertising. That included the money spent on TV ads, print ads, billboard ads, and so on. One of the brand goals of Nike was ubiquity. This means that advertising capital is spent on putting the Nike logo on all of the major athletes, in all different sports, as well as sponsoring major college and high school sports. It's hard if you're watching any sports game to miss a Nike logo. There is a very conscious effort by the company to ensure that the logo is everywhere and that it is broadcast widely. Primarily, Nike sends a common message: Just Do It. They send it through collaboration with a stable of sports stars through their massive campaigns.

Email and the Internet offered Nike a very different way to communicate. This was no longer broadcast but one-on-one *narrowcast*. In this effort, Nike saw the opportunity in email and a tool like EchoMail to accept inbound email and use its capability to understand the person's intentions from that email communication. They could segment the consumer by the attributes explained previously. Nike could thus track who someone was, what they wanted, and what their interests

were and proactively send out outbound communications targeted to those groups. For example, all the people who are into running and who liked their website may get a very different email than someone who was into baseball and wanted an internship. They could segment people in a way that was impossible to do through broadcast media. This is what is known as narrowcast, sending the right message to the right people at the right time.

Early adopters like Nike were great to work with because they saw email as not just a vehicle for transmitting information, but also as a tool for building bridges to multiple constituents. The opportunity to do that is available to every business, large or small, and personalized email is the ideal means. The key is to see personalized email not as a gimmick for manipulating customers, but as a way to generate an authentic connection.

Does the fact that the connection is with a software program rather than a flesh and blood person make it any less authentic? You'll need to decide that for yourself.

CHAPTER 12

Calvin Klein Makes You Wait

The Nike experience created a very close relationship between EchoMail and Wieden+Kennedy. Calvin Klein had approached Wieden+Kennedy in September 1998 to share advertising responsibilities for the CKOne unisex fragrance with their in-house agency. Historically, Calvin Klein had rarely outsourced any aspect of their image or brand building to outside agencies. It had always been done internally through their in-house agency CRK Advertising. However, Calvin Klein, seeing the power of email to connect from the Nike experience, was encouraged to potentially look at an agency to partner with that could similarly use email to build an intimate connection. In our discussions with the company, we learned that Calvin Klein, the designer himself, disliked the web; he thought the web was too dispersed and was not intimate. However, Calvin Klein loved email because it provided for one-to-one communication. He felt it was a thoughtful and an intimate medium, where someone in the comfort of their home could read an email and respond, at their own leisure.

Based on Calvin Klein's support of the email medium, we were offered the opportunity to do a ninety-day pilot to prove the value of email to support the brand-building efforts of a new product called CKOne, a unisex fragrance line for the Generation-Xers of the time, between the ages of thirteen to twenty. The task was to prove to Calvin Klein that email was a medium to build relationships with that group through electronic means. It was a tall order. However, the Nike experience had built confidence among the Wieden and EchoMail teams, on the power of email and integrated advertising.

Calvin Klein attracted people to the brand through their cutting edge TV and billboard advertising. But how could one leverage that to drive those same people to have an intimate conversation? Through a series of discussions, it was decided to use the various media in conjunction and in an integrative manner. This resulted in creating a prototype concept of a soap opera. The soap opera would contain three characters: Tia, Anna, and Robert. Tia was Robert's girlfriend and Anna was Robert's daughter, and Robert was in his late thirties. And clearly there was dynamics between Tia and Anna.

The first TV ad launched in a black-and-white, thirty-second mini-soap opera that exposed the dynamics of these three characters. The broadcast was limited to the United Kingdom. The ad ended on a cliffhanger. The only way one knew it was a Calvin Klein ad was it faded into the email addresses of each of the characters in black and white: tia@ckone.com, robert@ckone.com and anna@ckone.com. The unknown element was what would make viewers even write into these email

addresses. This was in 1998 and the number of email users was significantly fewer than what we have today.

People did write! EchoMail was used to analyze and sort the incoming email. As they came in, each email from the viewer was analyzed for its attitude, and for what kinds of issues they talked about. And in this case, unlike customer service issues or the issues for the president, the issues were about Robert's hair color, what gel he used or if they liked Tia's hair or what she was wearing. The emails were categorized by these different issues and responded to with a follow-up email, as a continuation of the soap opera, which Colin Dodd, the former scriptwriter for Michael Jackson's *Thriller*, had written. As email came in from people seeing the soap opera ad, they were segmented and follow-up soap opera dialogues were sent uniquely crafted for each character, via email. The conversation went from broadcast media to email.

In those first ninety days, hundreds of thousands of viewers sent emails and engaged with the three characters. These results were sufficient for Calvin Klein to fund another thirty-six-month period. The campaign went global. The advertisements were not only on television, but also on billboards. If you were in Times Square in New York City, you would see a big billboard with the picture of the soap opera character and their email address. By the second and third year, a total of sixteen characters, in addition to Tia, Robert, and Anna, were involved. In 2002 *Wired* magazine said this was the most revolutionary campaign in advertising history.

The press buzz on this campaign was massive. As *Wired* magazine wrote, "In 1998, a dozen beautiful men

and women began popping up on television, billboards, websites, and magazines in Europe and the United States. They were your typical, late-'90s beautiful people: Forlorn and apparently bored with their gorgeousness, they stared out at the world with a gaze that suggested thoughts that were either profound, or profoundly vacuous. It was not odd that these people looked somewhat mysterious—they were Calvin Klein fragrance models, models being a species that always appears to be a bit hard to figure out. What was odd, however, was that the ads— for Calvin Klein's signature fragrance, the 'unisex' CKOne—provided a then-novel way to peer into the enigma: an email address."

A common target of CKOne was a teenage guy or girl smitten by the model, who would then send a quick note to tia@ckone.com, anna@ckone.com, robert@ckone.com and/or any of the others, asking for information. In return, the teenager would get back a note that read like a letter to an old friend—it was personal, friendly, and it treated the reader as a confidante. For example, here's an excerpt from one of Anna's early letters. She begins, (note the lowercase) "survived but barely…"

> " i would have written sooner but i was scared my mom would walk in on my typing and catch me red-handed. she's gone off to the drugstore so i have about a half-hour window. you would not believe how screwed up an idea it was to have a party!!!!!!!"

The letter went on to describe how much Anna loves a certain unnamed "he," and she adds that if "you want nothing more to do with me, simply title your reply 'get lost' and I won't bother you anymore. Don't worry, I'm used to rejection." That "get lost" was a hip way to "opt out" or "unsubscribe," which ensured compliance with anti-SPAM regulations.

Every few days, another letter would come from Anna and the others, confiding more details from the characters' lives—whom they loved, whom they hoped to love, how their dream somehow always fell short of coming true. Characters invited the reader into a world of their own, with the aim of emotionally connecting with the readers. "In my head, I took the universal themes of love, lust, etc., and combined it with the most modern thing actually 'connecting us,' the Internet, and email specifically," wrote Kevin Drew Davis, the creative director at Wieden who worked on the campaign. "Ten characters, each writing to you as if you're their personal friend about what they were going through. But on a macro scale, each one of the characters was somehow connected to the others. Robert was Anna's father, and Robert was trying to have an affair with Tia. Anna lusted after Danny, and so forth.

Davis said, "It was supposed to be a discovery for the people who wrote in, and those first emails were great. They were asking a lot of questions about what this was." More than that, though, the campaign worked. "Hundreds of thousands of people went through the CKOne email," Davis wrote. Fragrance sales increased, and "because of the nature of the campaign and the time it was launched, it got a huge publicity. Some people

loved it, some people hated it. But isn't that every Calvin Klein campaign?"

Eventually, Calvin Klein stopped the print and TV spots, but they wanted the email "to just keep going and going," according to Colin Dodd, a 34-year-old fiction writer and bartender in Chapel Hill, North Carolina, who was contracted by the company to write the messages. Dodd had written a few short stories and had spent a long while turning one of his stories into a movie that wasn't getting made, "So I really needed the money," he said. "I was skeptical when I did it, and I thought it was going to take away all of my sensibilities. I was like, advertising—nothing but evil. But it was fun, and in the end it made me a better writer." And it's not hard to see how that happened. Over the three years, here's the story that developed, as described by Dodd:

"The initial story revolved around a commercial production company," Dodd started. "Robert was the director at the prod company, married to Patty, and they had a 15-year-old daughter named Anna, who had a crush on Danny, who was 18, who became a baseball player. Tia worked for Robert as a producer, and he fell in love with her and left his wife. Ian was production assistant and he fell in love with Tia, too, and he eventually won Tia away—or Tia eventually fell for Ian, although Ian had help from Kristy, who was his best friend, until they realized that they were in love." Also in the mix was Erica, a *femme fatale* who found herself in intimate situations with the other males.

Dodd said Calvin Klein laid down some ground rules for the characters—"no drinking, no drugs, no sex among the teenagers in the story"—but for three years,

he had a fair amount of creative freedom. The one thing that the campaign never did was plug the fragrance. "If you're talking about big brands like that, it's more important that you get the idea across, get an image across more than mention the scent," Dodd said. "So there were no passages like, 'Gosh, Tia smells so good.'"

Calvin Klein urged Dodd to keep the situations relatively open-ended, "on the premise that if there was uncertainty, people would keep coming back." In an email, Dodd added that people kept reading the messages because the characters kept revealing their secrets. "Email can have a confessional tone, and I tried to have one secret revealed per email. Anna hating her father, Ian loving his boss, Tia losing interest in Ian, Kristy hating New York ... the things they couldn't tell anyone else," he wrote. Indeed, by her final message, Anna seems genuinely touched by her conversations with the reader. "It's so weird and funny how sometimes it feels like something doesn't really happen to me until I get home and write it to you in an email and tell you about it," she writes.

Readers, too, were touched, Davis wrote. "The thing that impressed me most is that teenagers completely got it right away," Davis wrote. "For example, there was a group of school girls in the U.K. (several signups from the same school) who took on Anna as a personal friend. They would write things like, 'We know you're just a machine, but you need to watch out for Danny....' "They were letting the character in on what the other character had been saying to them. They were trying to direct the story! It was fantastic beyond my wildest expectations."

The Nike and Calvin Klein campaigns were a powerful example of where the email medium, integrated with an offline medium such as TV and print, explosively changed the nature of human interaction. Over 500 press articles were written about the CKOne campaign, generating a lot of brand buzz for Calvin Klein. What Calvin Klein received from this campaign was not just lists of email address contacts, but a whole buzz factor that they likely could not have received had they done broadcast advertising alone or email marketing alone. This integrative marketing was absolutely revolutionary and still is revolutionary today. The opportunity for marketers is to recognize that integrative marketing, combining broadcast media with narrowcast email, opens virgin areas of creative branding.

The Nike and CKOne experiences further reinforce the fact that email is a wonderful medium for conducting extended and intimate communication with a target audience, one-on-one. This is where the power of email truly is reflected. Email allows a company to communicate intimately using different strategies for different target groups of people, taking into account that particular person or group's interests and outlook. This ensures a much more personal level of communication, which results in higher appreciation by the individual or group being targeted, making them feel more connected and intimate.

The success of the Nike and CKOne projects resulted from establishing regular contact through targeted email communication with people who wanted an intimate communication that broadcast medium does not allow. Is it "good news" or "bad news" that email,

even with a commercial purpose, will now fill people's need for stories, insights, and at least some level of emotional connection?

The truth is, as the technology continues to advance the question of whether it's good or bad will be irrelevant. It's simply what's happening. Accept it if you wish, resist it if you can --but at least be aware of this new reality.

CHAPTER 13

Hilton Hotels Treats You Right

One of the key elements of a successful service organization is resolving problems correctly the first time. Nothing builds brand loyalty better than such first time resolution. You have a problem, you explain your problem and what your expectation of the resolution is, and it gets handled right the first time. Responsiveness builds trust, which leads to more sales and substantial goodwill, which spreads fast.

Email helps to accelerate both goodwill and its opposite. It's been said that a customer's negative phone and paper communication experience is relayed to five people. A Hewlett-Packard study revealed that a bad email customer experience is relayed to twenty-seven people. Resolving customer complaints on email, the first time, becomes even more crucial. If you take good care of customers when they complain, you not only make the customer happy that one time, but also get more business from them longer term.

Hilton Hotels' customer service teams understood this. Hilton saved money and actually got more business

from complaining customers. Their demonstrated quality of service proved that a complaint is a gift.

Hilton used email to handle a complaint as soon as it was raised. But more importantly, they knew it was economically prudent to resolve it the first time. Organizations like Hilton, for example, lose profits from a room if their customer service team takes more than one attempt to resolve a complaint. Furthermore, a customer whose complaint is resolved right the first time is very likely to be satisfied with the service and be willing to remain a long-term repetitive customer.

Hilton Hotels and Resorts is an international chain of hotels and resorts under the company Hilton Worldwide. Started by Conrad Hilton with one hotel in Texas in 1919, the Hilton brands now include hotels spread across eighty-four countries in six continents. Focusing on business travelers, leisure travelers, luxury resort guests, and popular destination visitors, Hilton is one of the most recognized brands in the world. The company headquarters is currently located in Tysons Corner, Virginia. Hilton Honors guest loyalty program is one of the largest of its kind with over twenty-nine million members and has developed a wide network partnering with airlines, car rental companies, credit card issuers, etc. With its range of loyalty membership, Hilton Honors is also a well-known brand across the world.

Hilton and Hilton Honors pride themselves about delivering a high level of customer service. With call centers located worldwide in locations such as Scotland, Texas, and the Philippines, the organization strives hard to deliver the best service to their guests all over the world on a twenty-four-hours-a-day, seven-days-a-week

basis. A reliable infrastructure based on advanced technology is essential for their customer service call centers to deliver this high level of service to their guests worldwide. They use different platforms for phone and email, having recognized that each medium is different. Hilton had experienced difficulties previously with certain poor choices in email management, having mistakenly thought that one platform could handle phone and email. Fortunately, Hilton learned from their mistakes. The technology team at Hilton worked hard to find the right email management solution to deliver on their brand promise of first time resolution. They selected EchoMail.

The key requirements for Hilton were the ability to support customer service agents located in multiple call centers in different parts of the world, the ability to route email written in different languages to different service teams, robust statistical analytics for real-time reporting for customer service team managers, and the ability to seamlessly integrate email data with other customer data stored elsewhere. Hilton's reason for these requirements was to ensure that they could deliver world-class email service. With EchoMail, Hilton was also able to increase productivity on the number of emails a customer service team responded per hour, while also providing accurate and prompt replies to their guests. This meant that instead of just receiving and closing emails fast, they also responded accurately, to achieve a high level of customer satisfaction.

One of Hilton's major needs was the ability to integrate a customer database with email management. Customer service agents wanted to see additional

information that was stored in the customer database at the instant and in the same screen they opened an email inquiry. Without this ability, when processing each email, the agents were spending extra time switching across different databases.

To make matters more complicated, customer database was managed at another location by a team outside of Hilton technology. A novel approach was designed to make the additional information visible to customer service agents by connecting email in the EchoMail platform to data in the external database systems. This integration improved the customer service agents' ability to read necessary information about the sender of the email, such as the guest's membership in Hilton Honors program, where the guest last stayed, and the length of the stay, for example. Not only did this additional information help the customer service agent to have all the necessary information in one screen, but also enabled the team to move customers with higher level of Honors loyalty membership to a separate queue with higher priority. Since membership in Diamond level of Honors were branded with better services such as faster reservation time, and quicker turnaround of service requests, this feature was reflected in the guest's ability to receive faster email response.

Customer service managers needed real-time and periodic reports to manage their representatives in each division. Real-time reports needed to provide accurate statistics on each representative's productivity, including up-to-the-minute work status. These real-time reports helped managers situated in Texas know what each representative was doing in any call center worldwide,

and reorganize email queue to achieve their quality of service levels. These periodic reports provided daily, weekly, and monthly statistics. This assisted mid- and senior-level managers to determine the effectiveness of their customer service organization. It is an incredible experience to observe how managers in the call center in Texas deliver email customer service in real-time, by dynamically reviewing and adjusting their teams.

Hilton was able to automatically route email to various service queues based on a variety of parameters. For example, information about the email sender's loyalty membership determined which queue that email was placed in—a high-priority queue or the standard queue. Information about the email sender's last stay such as which hotel and how many days, for example, determined which group within the email service team processed that email. In addition, each email's content was automatically analyzed for sensing the sender's attitude, the issues he or she wrote about, and any specific request, so as to identify additional factors to determine the right queue to route the email. This information also resulted in the customer service representative being presented with a suggested response, which made their response to the email faster and compliant with the standards set by Hilton. This implementation increased the number of emails each agent was able to process per hour, which is a key performance indicator of a successful customer service team.

The real-time reporting made a major difference in the instantaneous management of Hilton's worldwide customer service organization. Up-to-the-moment

information on emails pending to be processed, knowing which agents were currently on duty, and which agents were actively processing email (versus agents on break) were available to the managers. The hospitality industry in general is very sensitive to providing quick and accurate resolution to customer inquiries. This is not just prudent customer service practice; it also affects the hotel chain's bottom line. The up-to-the-moment information on service agents, routing of emails to appropriate agent queues, automatic analysis of emails, and selection of suggested responses based on the analysis, as well as additional information pulled from the customer database—all of them had a cumulative effect on the economics of Hilton's profitability.

When a guest makes a customer service call to Hilton, the call could cost Hilton a significant amount of money. This amount is more-or-less equal to the profit they make from an average room rental. So, 'single call closure' was a major factor for the Hilton customer service team. If multiple calls are made by a guest to resolve one inquiry, then Hilton loses a substantial amount of their revenue. The customer service team has to respond to emails in such a way that it really addresses the issue the first time. Integrating the customer database with email helped the service team to see the history of each guest's stay at Hilton, which improved the accuracy of response, avoiding "multiple email resolution."

Additional information from the customer database regarding the guest's last stay also helped the customer service team to upsell the guest through follow-up targeted messages. In the email response, the guest is informed about their rewards program and how the

guest could earn more rewards by taking certain action. This was a timely way to integrate marketing and service. Furthermore, this approach helped Hilton to establish their brand presence with guests, since the responses were not simply resolution of a question the guest had raised. The responses also provided additional information - a soft sell that was targeted and personalized to the guest.

CHAPTER 14

NPR Sells You News

National Public Radio (NPR) is the world's first non-commercial satellite delivered radio network, it is an internationally acclaimed producer and distributor of non-commercial news, talk and entertainment programming. NPR is a privately supported not-for-profit membership organization. Interestingly, NPR is not a radio station by itself nor does NPR own a radio station. But it supports 760 independently operated, non-commercial public radio stations spread all over the 50 states of the country through satellite.

These stations combine NPR's offerings with local programming to make it more interesting to local listeners. NPR's mission is to work with member stations to create a better-informed public, challenged and invigorated by a deeper understanding about the world around us. NPR also distributes content through other media such as CD's, books, the Internet and the Sirius satellite studio.

NPR although a non-profit enterprise, was aware that it was in an extremely competitive business. Today's

radio listeners have access to an increasingly high number and variety of programs broadcast by a number of radio stations to choose from. In this highly competitive atmosphere NPR had to create a loyal listener base by making its programs preferred over others because only a large listenership would get the advertisers to consider it as a medium of mass reach and bring in the advertising revenues. NPR realized that this was possible only through a better understanding of public tastes and preferences and a constant dialog with them. In view of its large and a countrywide listener base it decided that electronic communication would be the most ideal and cost effective medium to reach out to them.

NPR realized that it did not have the time or expertise to handle the huge volume of mail that would be involved in an exercise of this nature and wanted to tie up with a professional email management agency. It chose EchoMail as its Email Relationship Marketing Agency.

EchoMail analyzed the situation and deployed its Direct Marketing (DM) and Customer Care (CC) tools. DM was meant to communicate to its large listener base on NPR's plans, forthcoming programs, and generally maintain a dialogue. CC was deployed to receive, analyze, segregate and route the large number of incoming mail to the relevant departments and generate rapid and relevant response.

EchoMail helped NPR in sending highly customized and targeted campaigns, which helped in bringing its listener base closer to their favorite radio network and bringing in new listeners by creating interest among

potential listeners. It informed them on its future plans, new programs in the pipeline and sought their views. CC helped in analyzing the feedback generated by the huge volume of inbound mail and helped in gauging listener taste, preferences, how they perceived NPR, popularity of its programs and tailor programs accordingly. It also categorized incoming mail and routed them to the relevant departments and facilitated speedy response. A better understanding of listener preference helped NPR to evolve into a more listener friendly radio network. Prompt response to listener mail gave it an image of being responsive and sensitive to listener sentiments.

This, along with the inclusion of popular programs enabled by a better understanding of listener tastes, helped NPR retain its loyal listener base and bring in new listeners in a highly competitive atmosphere. NPR is a unique organization. Because much of the programing consists simply of human voices talking to one another in informal tones, people experience listening to NPR as a genuinely "human" experience. Any message from NPR needs to be aligned with that experience.

Every business owner should take that lesson to heart. There's nothing to be gained from building a brand identity and then undercutting it with incongruent communication.

CHAPTER 15

Even Small Guys Want Your Friendship

Small and mid-market businesses can learn a great deal from the work of large organizations. Email has grown to be the preferred channel for most people when it comes to business communications, especially when the business is transacted online. The United States alone has over twenty-seven million small and medium business (SMB) organizations. These include one-person businesses as well as those organizations with less than 500 full-time employees. Even though small and medium businesses have fewer employees and may have smaller assets, most of the activities involved in the business process of SMBs are the same as large enterprises.

An SMB, like any company, has to obtain customers, vendors, and service providers; hire, train, and manage employees; produce and deliver products and services; and maintain customer relations. SMBs, like large companies, also need to establish communication with their customers to keep them and get new ones. And email is one of the best SMB channels of communication for both marketing and customer service. Even though

an SMB may receive and send fewer emails as compared with a large enterprise, there is still a need for strategies, best practices, and tools to effectively manage email within SMBs. The lessons from large enterprises can be extremely valuable in this regard.

Unlike large organizations, however, SMBs can benefit from email with far less investment. SMBs' requirements are less rigid and less specialized compared with large enterprises. SMBs' data transmission, security, and storage needs, for example, are more generic as compared with the big guys. This means that SMBs can gain significant value from email communications by simply replicating some of the best strategies, practices, and techniques, like the ones used by big brands, as we have discussed in the earlier chapters of this part of the book.

As with other organizations, whether large or small, there are two main areas in which email can provide great value to SMBs: inbound email management and outbound email marketing. Inbound email management focuses on the receipt of customer inquiries, taking proper action to address their issues, and responding to customers in a timely manner. Outbound email marketing includes organizing customer email lists, creating attractive messages and offers, proactively connecting with customers, and tracking the customer interaction to understand what kinds of communication worked, and what did not.

From large organizations, we have learned about using email for managing crisis, maintaining good customer relations, managing account information, enhancing guest and member relations, ensuring prompt,

trusted and safe communications, creating a comfortable environment for donors and children, managing sales leads, being compliant, and managing events. Similarly, we learned how large enterprises were able to use email to reach their constituents using integrated marketing, multichannel marketing, personalized marketing for mobilizing at the grassroots level, and conducting consumer behavior surveys, all the while ensuring secure data storage, data integration, and centralized and decentralized message control.

SMBs, like large enterprises, are continuing to receive growing volumes of inbound email each day from their customers. Creating a trusted communication channel for such questions and complaints to be handled promptly and communicated back is a significant part of good email customer care, whether the business is small or large. Volume of inbound email, however, is not the driving reason for implementing email management. In fact, even in large organizations, whether the volume was small or large, the motivating factor in implementing email management, which many find surprising, was to build accountability between the customer and the company.

Consider an SMB such as Taco John's, a smaller Mexican fast food chain in the Midwest. For Taco John's, it was clear that although the number of emails each day was not that many, according to their chief financial officer, their objective was to provide prompt response to each email and take accountability for each issue. That was part of their business or brand promise.

Commitment to such a promise required Taco John's to strategize and create a methodology using EchoMail

to route incoming inquiries to both the local restaurant that was referred to in the incoming email, as well as to the internal centralized customer service team. Taco John's, moreover, wanted to keep track of the statistics on the issues and locations so they could identify patterns and address issues before they became a bigger crisis. For example, if a particular restaurant consistently got lots of complaints, this would be an early warning signal to Taco John's headquarters to intervene and make the necessary adjustments.

The key elements of the Taco John's example are that even though email volume was low, they wanted to make sure each email was:

1. Received and categorized
2. Routed to the right person;
3. Received a prompt and proper response
4. Tracked to ensure service levels
5. Viewed as a window on trends or patterns of communication

Any SMB can implement all of the above elements of inbound email management to ensure a solid email customer service program. Such an effort will serve to retain existing customers as well as build customer loyalty.

Outbound email marketing includes the ability for an organization to disseminate information about their company and its products or services using email. One way is to simply broadcast one email message to all. Alternatively, another way is to send personalized and targeted email via multiple channels, motivating recipients to take action within the email, which may

include responding back and tracking all the various actions, while ensuring that data from all sources are integrated and securely maintained. Such capabilities are now readily available in many email marketing services such as EchoMail and others.

Growing numbers of SMBs use outbound email marketing every day. This includes nonprofits, law offices, recruiters, artists, and small to medium financial service providers, to name a few. All of these organizations are able to take advantage of the same great features and functionality that large organizations have used, such as anti-SPAM compliance, secure data storage, data integration, personalized and targeted messaging, event management and surveys and questionnaires. Above all, email marketing enables them, unlike print advertising, to track their investment to the penny and make real-time changes to a marketing program. Such accountable use of marketing dollars is a significant advantage for SMBs with email marketing.

SMB organizations have email communication requirements very similar to the requirements of much larger companies. The lessons learned from large enterprises are applicable to SMB organizations. Two important applications for SMBs are inbound email management for supporting customer retention and loyalty, and outbound email marketing for acquiring new customer sales.

These days I'm especially interested in working with small and mid-range business. My reasons are both practical and political. Small and mid-range companies are of course a huge market that I'm eager to access. I also know that use of powerful new technologies should

not be limited to the wealthiest and largest corporations, nor to agencies of government and law enforcement. In the 21st century, this is what "power to the people" has come to mean.

CHAPTER 16

Bush Versus Gore

During the 2000 presidential election campaign, George W. Bush was generally portrayed as less intellectually sophisticated than Al Gore. Whether or not that was accurate, Bush definitely ran a smarter campaign. Bush's people at least knew what they didn't know, and they did know what they wanted to do.

The success of the Bush for President Campaign lay in connecting people at a grassroots level. Led by direct mail expert Karl Rove, the Bush campaign committee knew the power of mobilizing people at the grassroots. They learned that email communication is very personal and can be used as an excellent tool for one-to-one communication.

The campaign team had a conscious strategy to collect email addresses of as many individuals as possible in each precinct and establish targeted one-on-one email conversation with them. The campaign team identified with the "personal" nature of email, and used it to mobilize the power of grassroots supporters ultimately to win primaries and eventually the general election,

which made George W. Bush the president of the United States of America.

As everyone knows, the 2000 presidential election was very close. Bush won by the thinnest of margins. The election was noteworthy for the controversy that awarded Florida's 25 electoral votes to Bush, the subsequent recount process in that state, and the unusual event of the winning candidate having received fewer popular votes than the runner-up. Although the campaign focused mainly on domestic issues such as the projected budget surplus, proposed reforms of Social Security and Medicare, health care, and competing plans for tax relief, foreign policy was often the most important issue. As the election night wore on, the returns in a handful of small to medium-size states, including Wisconsin and Iowa, were extremely close; however, it was the state of Florida that would make clear the winner of the election. As the final national results were tallied the following morning, Bush had clearly won a total of 246 electoral votes, while Gore had won 255 votes.

Two hundred and seventy votes were needed to win. Two smaller states - New Mexico (5 electoral votes) and Oregon (7 electoral votes) - were still too close to call. It was Florida (25 electoral votes), however, that the news media focused their attention on. Mathematically, Florida's 25 electoral votes became the key to an election win for either candidate.

Although both New Mexico and Oregon were declared in favor of Gore over the next few days, Florida's statewide vote took center stage because that state's winner would ultimately win the election. The

outcome of the election was not known for more than a month after the balloting ended because of the extended process of counting and then recounting Florida's presidential ballots. After an intense recount process, then Governor George W. Bush was officially declared the winner of Florida's electoral votes and, as a result, the entire presidential election. The process was extremely divisive, and led to calls for electoral reform in Florida.

Bush's platform had included compassionate conservatism, tax breaks for all, and a humble foreign policy with no nation building, "No Child Left Behind" education policy, energy policy including initiatives for use of conserving technologies as well as decreasing foreign dependence on oil through increased domestic production, and redesign of the military with emphasis on super-modern hardware, flexible tactics, and less international deployment. Gore's platform included safe and legal abortion defending women's right to choose, continuation of Clinton's economic policies with limited tax breaks for working families, improvements to equal rights and opportunities - be it based on gender, race, sexual orientation or disabilities, wider separation of church and state, transformation of educational system including more teachers, improved classrooms, increased public education and tuition savings program, energy policy emphasizing use of new technology and strong control on global warming factors, strong agenda in foreign policy including leadership in response to violence and vigorous intervention abroad and a strong push on technology, including policies supporting free-market Internet.

The 2000 presidential campaign proved every vote counts. Hardworking supporters won each vote at the grassroots level through a door-to-door campaign. Any advantage could have a significant effect. Jeanniey Mullen, a business development executive at EchoMail, recognized there was an opportunity to use email for the presidential campaigns. Initially, she approached the Democrats thinking that if Al Gore "invented the Internet," his team would definitely want to use email for the campaign. However, something interesting took place.

The campaign leaders at the Democratic Party were arrogant. They felt they knew everything about email and discounted it as real channel. They did not think email was significant. They were going to use other types of media, including the web, but not email. This was quite a letdown for Jeanniey.

Not giving up, Jeanniey approached the Bush campaign team. She noticed something significantly different. The Bush campaign led by Karl Rove, who some consider as the "Devil," was actually very open. The Bush campaign was willing to explore new ideas. They wanted to learn how to really use email at the grassroots, and saw it as a one-on-one medium that integrated with their one-on-one philosophy of connecting with ordinary folks.

The Bush campaign was smarter than the Gore campaign. They knew what they didn't know. They wanted to use email to add muscle to their grassroots tactics. They were interested and curious to learn, and EchoMail provided them opportunities to let them know how email could be used in the presidential campaign.

EchoMail gave them examples of what they did with Calvin Klein, Nike, and the White House—and emphasized that email could be used as a vehicle to engage their "customers" at a one-to-one level, in an intimate manner.

In their case, the one-to-one communication would prove crucial to raise donations. And to get people in the neighborhood excited about rallying behind the cause. The campaign team achieved this through viral email marketing. Viral email encouraged one recipient to forward the email to another.

This was a very new concept that few were exploring at the time, and Karl Rove, who had built his entire career on direct mail business and knew the power of grassroots marketing, saw viral marketing as a fast way to build new connections—far cheaper than with print and postal mail. His team was therefore quickly able to understand the power of email and began to gather email lists and addresses.

The Bush Campaign also targeted its bank of nearly 200,000 wealthy supporters and used the same viral process with them. They sent a series of targeted weekly email marketing campaign programs. In those email marketing campaigns, the recipients were encouraged to participate in receiving ongoing newsletters. The recipients were given up-to-date information on what Bush was doing, where he was campaigning, what he had said, and so on. The purpose of that consistent communication was to build an intimate relationship with each of the Bush supporters. Responses were also answered in a timely manner, and those responses always encouraged forwarding the email to others.

The Bush campaign team had an elaborate strategy for volunteers to go door-to-door in their local neighborhoods. The volunteers visited each home with multiple objectives. Get the neighbor as an active volunteer or get the neighbor as a donor. Each visiting volunteer was encouraged to collect as many email addresses as possible from their daily visits. At the end of the day, they would return to the field offices with their laptops that had the information they had collected. The information in the laptops would be uploaded to campaign headquarters.

This is an area where the campaign team faced multiple challenges. In the year 2000, Internet technology was not as developed as it is today and wireless technology for public access, especially, was in its nascent stages. This made uploading of the data from field offices extremely hard. Sometimes it would take hours for the data from some of the remote locations to upload. When it came to the day an email campaign was scheduled, it could get very complex with synchronization of data from different locations.

With anti-SPAM rules developing, even in 2000, data had to be properly synchronized, so that a recipient's request to be removed from the mailing list was met promptly, especially in a scenario like an election where one does not want the person to get upset on a simple matter like opting out of an email campaign. With the data upload, synchronization of the data, and opt-out status updates all taking place, sending an email campaign at the predetermined time required near perfect orchestration—and the Bush team lived up to the task. Today, this is made far easier technologically;

however, the commitment and need to integrate multiple databases and connect them together, like the Bush campaign had done with lesser technology, is still not fully realized by many organizations.

Another concern was information security. With information of people all over the nation, especially donors to the election, a lot of emphasis was placed on secure transfer of information from field offices to campaign headquarters to our facility. Even though they did not store any payment-specific information such as bank account or credit card numbers, personal information was still very important and best security measures available at the time were employed to securely maintain the exchange of data. Dispersed nationwide, collecting such campaign data in a decentralized manner, and using grassroots teams made this project very different from corporate customers.

The recipients of Bush campaign email were also segmented. This was particularly important in certain districts where precinct-by-precinct, block-by-block, is how the election was going to be determined. Different areas, therefore, were sent targeted and customized content. For example, places like Ohio and Florida, as we all know now, ended up being highly contested. Those areas got very different information than the other parts of the country.

Over the course of the campaign, the Bush for President team raised a significant part of their campaign fund through the use of email. They signed up huge numbers of new donors through the process of targeted viral email connecting the grassroots, door-to-door, as well as their wealthy donors.

We cannot definitively say that Bush's winning the presidential election was because of email. But it is likely that the email effort provided a huge advantage, particularly in those hard-fought districts such as Ohio and Florida. What would have happened if Gore had also embraced email? The Obama campaign of 2008 took many lessons from Bush's effective use of email. They hired specialists just for managing email communication and to build a similar integrated grassroots model as Bush had done—and it clearly worked for them.

At a time when many underestimated email, the George W. Bush campaign did not. Though considered by some as not the most intelligent candidate, Bush appointed smart folks to run his campaign, folks who had recognized the power of one-to-one marketing and embraced email.

This attitude of being open to email, as a new medium, and exhibiting a willingness to learn its nuances and particular usage, is what gave the Bush campaign an important advantage over the Democrats, who did not value the email medium and thought the web by itself was sufficient for their traditional campaign activities. George Bush's campaign proved the power of viral email marketing, combined with door-to-door grassroots campaign, to not only reach voters but also to build deeper connections, reinforced by email and face-to-face communications.

George W. Bush's ascent to the presidency taught one of the most basic lessons of winning elections: all politics are local. The Bush campaign focused at the grassroots, collecting email addresses door-to-door, and

communicating relevant messages, face-to-face and through email, with targeted content.

PART 4

Freedom Now

*Email has now become a true AI technology,
with applications in politics as well as commerce.
There's no getting away from it. So what is to be done?*

CHAPTER 17

The Conundrum

The USPS is the connective tissue of American democracy. As a systems biologist, I know that the connective tissue of the body is essential for life. The connective tissue stands at the interface of our physical, mental, and emotional selves. It allows us to convert what we sense in our environment to responsive action. Without it, we are nothing.

The USPS is a core part of our social connective tissue. Its destruction means that we as a social organism will cease to have an essential and important functional element for our sensing, movement, and responsiveness. Bit by bit, parts of the USPS have been gutted. The premium parts have been taken away and privatized. What remains are the spoils.

As this has taken place, email volume has grown explosively, overtaking postal mail as early as 1997. The USPS should have embraced email and provided an infrastructure of mail services in electronic form, thereby renewing itself and its deteriorating connective tissue.

But, as I described earlier, the management at USPS did not have the vision or the courage to do that

Today, email is the medium of choice over first class letters. However, nearly all of our email is not private. Individuals and private companies can access it anytime. We have implicitly traded our rights for "free" email services that at any point can be shut down or used against us.

When Hosni Mubarak, the Egyptian dictator, shut down all electronic messaging throughout the country, this was accomplished through Vodafone, a private company with accountability only to its shareholders. There was not even a pretense that a basic public right had been eliminated. The shutdown could be portrayed as simply a business matter.

This is dangerous. Electronic communication has been like a genie in a bottle. It has given us so many things that in the past we could only have wished for – but it has also created a dependency that has come to dominate our lives. The USPS mail system, governed by a body of law dating back to the framing of the Constitution, stipulates that mail will not be tampered with. But email can be tampered with anytime and anyplace, and in many different ways. It can change not only what we write or read, but even who and what we are.

I first had a premonition of this in 1994. I woke in the middle of the night with a very unexpected thought. Maybe it had been part of a dream, I don't recall. What I do remember is a sudden awareness that someday I would be sitting across a table from a robot, or talking

on the phone with one, and that I might be completely unaware of that fact.

Why did that thought seem so startling? It was the kind of scene that was often depicted in science fiction novels, and I had read dozens of them.

Looking back on it now, my thought about robot realization may actually have been a screen for another, deeper thought – one that I mentioned in the introduction to this book.

It's the thought that I myself might be a robot, and might have become one by a process wholly outside my awareness. And I don't mean that as a metaphor. I mean that I, and perhaps many others, could transform into a completely programmable entity who is as much a "machine" as anything other than a machine. It's that simple.

I hope the chapters of this book have shown you how mere email messages can be valuable sources of information for corporations and government. I hope you've also seen how corporations and government can use that information to precisely target you in a reply. So precisely, in fact, that you will be certain it was not a machine but an actual flesh and blood human being who sat down and typed that message just for you. Most importantly, you will respond to that fully-automated message exactly as planned by the sender. You will have just the right thoughts and feelings, and you will do just what is expected of you. You will be fully automated.

This too is a quite common motif in science fiction. Robots, much to their own surprise, discover what they are and what they aren't. What was so striking, therefore,

about my thought that night in 1994 was not that it was original but that it was already true, or soon could be.

My objection to this is not a moral one. Once certain technologies became available – including email, which has become a sub-category of artificial intelligence – it's useless and childishly sentimental to whine about this being "wrong." If something can be done, it will be done – especially when it can be done by billion dollar companies and bank-dominated governments.

Without whining, then, we still must ask ourselves what is to be done in a world where technology is not just powerful and pervasive, but actually transformative of who and even what we are.

All the great mechanical inventions have long since been invented. No one is going to discover the wheel again, or build the first bicycle. All the big changes from now on – and there will be a lot of them – will have artificial intelligence as their foundation. This will basically eliminate what we now call privacy, which as we have discussed, was something that the Founding Fathers were determined to protect through the postal mail system.

Perhaps privacy is not even a strong enough word here. The interface with artificial intelligence will not involve merely protecting information. It will go far beyond just keeping secrets. It will literally be a matter of preserving one's autonomy as an individual human being versus an exquisitely perfected integration with AI – an integration in which the distinction between man and machine becomes so hopelessly old fashioned that for practical purposes it ceases to exist.

And there is no going back. The Luddite inclination to throw away all the cell phones and laptops is not going to work. It's much too late for that. Anyway, maybe it's time for people to change into machines. Maybe that's the next evolutionary stage -- the weird spin on Marxist dialectic that I suggested in the Introduction to this book. Instead of running away from their cast iron machines, today's proletariat can merge with their plastic ones.

There is so much mystery about what's happening now that I can't really say I have an answer to the many questions. As a revolutionary myself, I always try to draw revolutionary conclusions from any circumstance. In this situation, it's clear that those in power are not listening to us. Hillary and the Clinton's, and the ruling of the FBI, make it loud and clear: we have rigged system. The elites get private servers, beyond observation so they can have deniability. We, the masses, get bogus "free" email that are watched and observed moment by moment.

On top of all this, the data being collected on us, and AI technologies like EchoMail, only affordable by the elites, are being used to predict our behavior and control us. In short, email the medium which was created for equality and collaboration, while ensuring privacy, has been subverted. I take this very personally.

The good news is this: you now are aware of it. And, awareness is critical to change a situation. So, what is to be done?

CHAPTER 18

What Is To Be Done?

We can change the current situation and regain our freedom, if we act. There are three things in particular that need to done.

First, the USPS or other postal services in democratic countries, such as America and India, must be forced to implement truly free email. By free email, this means that every email we send is OUR email. No one else owns it. No one can read it, either by humans or Google-like algorithms to market to us, without our permission. No email during transmission can be tampered with. If an email is tampered with, legal and criminal penalties will be imposed, as they are now with postal mail. Since private companies today own your email, and you "willingly" signed up for those "free" services, without a public alternative, you have no legal recourse to email tampering.

Second, we should never allow what occurred in Egypt and Turkey, take place again. In both these situations, the dictators of these countries simply made phone calls to the CEOs of major telecommunication

companies, during mass uprisings, to shutdown email communications. This would be like the U.S. President calling the Postmaster General and shutting down all postal mail communications. The Founding Fathers established a governance system and legal framework that legally prohibits the President from taking that action.

However, when it comes to email, this is not the case. There is only one way to avoid such a scenario: we as the public must either seize control of existing private telecommunication networks or have our own public telecommunication networks, like the public highway system. I favor the latter, which, fortunately, is now possible with recent technological advances that enable us as public citizens, to create our own public networks, owned and operated by us, and supported by our tax dollars.

Third, in spite of sloganeering, including Google's famous "Do No Evil," evidence shows private companies including Google actively collaborate and collude with governments to share what should be private. However, because they are private companies, they are allowed to do so, particularly since the vast majority of people (who cannot afford private email servers like Hillary) unwittingly sign away their rights when they subscribe to the "free" email service.

How do we end such collusion? Large companies such as Google and Facebook, which control critical communication across billions of people, should become public utilities. That transformation should take place once the companies reach a certain scale. The criteria for

determining at what point the transformation takes place, should be defined and legislated by a public itself.

These three demands are critical to the fulfillment of our freedom not only for the future of email but also for the future of the world as a whole.